PAINLESS
American
Government

Jeffrey Strausser
illustrated by Denise Gilgannon

BARRON'S

T 109555

All inquiries should be addressed to:
Barron's Educational Series, Inc.
250 Wireless Boulevard
Hauppauge, New York 11788
http://www.barronseduc.com

Library of Congress Catalog Card No. 2003056092

ISBN-13: 978-0-7641-2601-7
ISBN-10: 0-7641-2601-6

Library of Congress Cataloging-in-Publication Data

Strausser, Jeffrey.
   Painless American government / Jeffrey Strausser ; illustrated
by Denise Gilgannon.
      p.   cm.
   Includes bibliographical references and index.
   ISBN 0-7641-2601-6
   1. United States–Politics and government.   I. Title.
JK275S77 2004
320.473–dc21   2003056092

PRINTED IN CANADA
9 8 7 6 5

CONTENTS

To Beth, Katie, and Matthew

INTRODUCTION

What this book will do for you

Many students are a bit confused—maybe, even a lot confused—about the structure of our government and the way it works. That's where this book can help you. Rather than have to wade through thick textbooks that seem to have everything in them except what you want to know, you can learn about American government painlessly. This book provides concise and easy-to-read, interesting descriptions of all the important areas of government. For example, you will learn about the Declaration of Independence and the Constitution, the three branches of government, civil liberties and civil rights, and elections. Simple and clear charts will take you through how Congress makes laws and how our courts of law work to seek justice for all Americans.

Each chapter explains an important area of government, so if you want to learn about a particular area, you need check out only one chapter. On the other hand, if you prefer to learn about everything, you can read the book from cover to cover. You'll be an expert on American government before you know it!

As you read, you will come across some words that might be unfamiliar to you. Each possibly unfamiliar word is boldfaced, set in red, italicized, and defined, so you won't have to lug a dictionary around with you!

Every chapter has several short and fun exercises to help you review its material. The "Minute with Senator WordSmart" exercises will help you review new words. "The Choice is Yours" is a series of short multiple-choice exercises that will check your understanding of the chapter's key concepts.

Finally, for Internet surfers, each chapter contains Web addresses (URLs) where you can find additional information about topics discussed in the chapter. It is not necessary to refer to these sites, because each chapter topic is concisely, yet thoroughly explained within the pages of the chapter. However, if surfing through the ocean of cyberspace is fun for you, just look for the *Surf's up* box and check out the Web pages listed there.

Web addresses change!

You should be aware that addresses on the World Wide Web are constantly changing. Although every attempt has been made to provide you with the most current addresses available, the nature of the Internet makes it virtually impossible to keep track of the many changes that seem to occur on a daily basis.

If you should come across a Web address that no longer appears to be valid, either because the site no longer exists or because the address has changed, don't panic. Simply do a *key word search* on the subject matter in question. For example, if you are interested in finding out more about the Bill of Rights and the particular address appears to be invalid, do a search for various words related to the Bill of Rights. These are the key words. A **key word search** for this topic might include, for example, "freedom of speech." If an initial key word search provides too many potential sites, you can always narrow down the number of choices by doing a second key word search that will limit your original search to only those sites that contain the terms for both your first and second searches.

WARNING: Not every response to your search will match your criteria, and some sites may contain adult material. If you are ever in doubt, check with someone who can help you.

CHAPTER ONE

What Is Government?

OLIGARCHY

AUTOCRACY

FOR THE PEOPLE... BY THE PEOPLE

DEMOCRACY

WHO GOVERNS?

We can think of **government** as the institutions and their systems that rule a country and its people. Simply put: *To govern is to rule.*

A government can be one of three types:

- an autocracy
- an oligarchy
- a democracy.

An **autocracy** is a government controlled by a single individual—a dictator, for example. By comparison, in an **oligarchy**, rather than a single ruler, small, powerful groups of landowners, military officers, or wealthy businesspeople control the government institutions. Finally, if more people participate in the governing process and have some influence over decision-making, the government is a **democracy**. Our government is a democracy, and because it is, let's look at this kind of government more closely.

DEMOCRACY: THEN AND NOW

The most important feature of democracy is that it is a government whose citizens grant it the authority to rule. The word *democracy* comes from two Greek words: *demos* (the people) and *kratos* (rule or power). Therefore, democracy means the people, together, rule themselves. They aren't ruled by one person as in an autocracy, or by a few people as in an oligarchy. Although ours is a democracy, if you look in the Appendix of this book and read the Declaration of Independence or the Constitution, you won't find the word *democracy* in either of these important documents. Does that mean the founders of our country were unaware of democracy as a government?

Actually, they knew about democracy, and they didn't like it. At the time of the founding of our nation, people spoke of democracy in a negative way. Democracy had come to mean a government run by crowds of people, a government that ignored laws, and a government that provided little protection for its citizens. The founders had read about the system of democracy that had been popular in ancient Athens and a few other Greek city-states for a short period. Greek citizens would meet in large groups to discuss problems, pass laws, and decide other matters necessary to run their country. These city-states didn't last long, however, because as their population grew and they needed their government to do more, their system couldn't handle it. There were so many different opinions about what action was needed and who should do it that nothing could be decided. Because no one was in charge, the cities became unruly; they resorted to mob rule and, finally, to dictators. We learned a lesson from this painful start for democracy.

We are now careful to distinguish between the *direct democracy* of Athens and the other Greek city-states where each person had an equal and *direct* say in the government, and the system of democracy that we have today in the United States. When we talk about democracy today, we mean representative democracy. *Representative democracy* is a system of government in which the people elect certain individuals to *represent* their opinions, concerns, and desires within the government. Plato, a learned man who lived in ancient Greece, gave us another term for this type of democracy—a *republic*.

A Minute with Senator WordSmart
Set # 1

Take a minute to make sure that you understand the meanings of the new words. Match the word in the left-hand column with its definition in the right-hand column by drawing a line from the word to its definition. If you want to check your work, review the Answer Key in the back of the book.

1. Government

2. Autocracy

3. Oligarchy

4. Democracy

5. Direct democracy

6. Representative democracy

7. Republic

a. A government in which the people, together, rule themselves.

b. A system of government in which the people elect certain individuals to represent their opinions, concerns, and desires within the government.

c. The institutions and their systems that rule a country and its people.

d. A government controlled by a small group of powerful people.

e. Each person has an equal and direct say in the government.

f. Another name for a representative democracy.

g. A government that is controlled by a single individual.

Did You Know?

The word *republic* comes from the Latin word *res publica*, which means "public matters."

The Choice Is Yours
Set # 1

To check your understanding of the previous material, answer the following questions by selecting the letter of the correct answer. If you want to check your work, refer to the Answer Key in the back of the book.

1. Which type of government is led by a dictator?
   a. A democracy
   b. An oligarchy
   c. An autocracy
   d. None of the above

2. The United States has a _____ democracy.
   a. direct
   b. authoritarian
   c. representative
   d. Greek

3. Another name for our type of democracy is _____.
   a. a republic
   b. a city-state
   c. an oligarchy
   d. an autocracy

4. _____ are ruled by small groups of powerful people.
   a. Democracies
   b. Autocracies
   c. Oligarchies
   d. Republics

5. The word *democracy* appears in _____.
   a. the Constitution
   b. the Declaration of Independence
   c. the Constitution and the Declaration of Independence
   d. neither the Constitution nor the Declaration of Independence

HOW THEY GOVERN

Besides differing in *who* governs, governments also differ in *how* they govern. ***Totalitarian governments*** exercise complete control over the people; those in authority have unlimited power and don't have to answer to anyone. By comparison, ***authoritarian governments*** have their power limited by a group, such as the military, religious groups, labor unions, or a combination of all three. Both types of government rarely concern themselves with the desires of their citizens; they rule as much as their power will let them. Finally, in the United States and in many other nations, a framework of written laws limits representatives as to how and over what matters they can have control. Governments limited by a formal framework of laws that outline its functions and powers (usually referred to as a ***constitution***) are called ***constitutional governments***. A copy of our Constitution is in the Appendix of this book. Our government follows the laws written in our Constitution while operating as a democracy; thus, our system of government is a ***constitutional democracy***.

Surf's up...

If you want to learn more about the different kinds of governments, glide into this site:

apgovernment.com/apgovernment/sourcesofgovt.html

A Minute with Senator WordSmart
Set # 2

Take a minute to make sure you understand the meanings of the new words by matching the word or phrase with its definition.

1. Totalitarian government

   a. A government limited by a framework of laws.

2. Authoritarian government

   b. A government whose power is only limited by a few powerful groups.

3. Constitution

   c. Our system of government.

4. Constitutional government

   d. A formal framework of laws that outlines the functions and powers of the government.

5. Constitutional democracy

   e. A government whose power has no limits.

OUR IDEALS

Our constitutional democracy works because the citizens of our country believe in certain ideals—that is, we have agreed to live by the following:

- We accept *majority rule*. This means we agree to let each person have a say in the form of a vote, and we agree to follow the course of action that received the most votes.
- Although we accept majority rule, we agree that the rights of the people who were in the *minority* (the group with less people in it than the majority) must be protected. Our rights and freedoms are for all people.

- We want to be ruled by laws, not powerful individuals. We also want all citizens to be treated fairly by these laws.
- We want *freedom of speech*—that is, we want to be allowed to question and criticize our elected officials for the purpose of improving our government.
- We want our government to serve the people, not the other way around. Every government has a source of sovereignty or authority. In previous centuries, the source of sovereignty in many countries was the monar-

chy—the king. However, Americans place the source of authority in the people; therefore, the government must respect and follow the will of the people. We call this *popular sovereignty*.

Things to Think About

1. Why is it better to live in a country ruled by laws rather than one ruled by a few powerful people?
2. Why is freedom of speech essential to a democracy?
3. In what ways does your government serve you? How could it do a better job?
4. What are the advantages and disadvantages of majority rule?
5. Why is it important to protect the rights and freedoms of the people in the minority?

I know of no safe repository of the ultimate powers of the society but the people themselves and if we think them not enlightened enough to exercise their control with a wholesome discretion, the remedy is not to take it from them but to inform their discretion.

—Thomas Jefferson (1820)

> ## Projects You Can Do
>
> 1. Use your local library or the Internet to find an example of a country that is:
>
>   - a democracy
>   - an oligarchy
>   - an autocracy.
>
>   Which people in government have the power in each country?
>
> 2. As a class, create and govern yourselves as:
>
>   - an autocracy
>   - an oligarchy
>   - a democracy.
>
>   What problems arose with each system?

MAKING OUR CONSTITUTIONAL DEMOCRACY WORK

We have set up our government so that it can support the ideals that we mentioned in the previous section. We want our government to be strong so that both our own citizens and foreign countries will respect it; however, we don't want it to be so powerful that it endangers our freedoms and rights. The first way we accomplish this goal is through a fair system of representation.

In a representative democracy, the people delegate (lend) their authority to their elected representatives. To earn the right to represent us, these officials must first become **candidates** in an **election**, which is a formal process in which the people select or **vote** for their representatives. The candidate winning the most votes within a group becomes the representative. In the United States, candidates compete for the presidency, the vice presidency, the Senate, and the House of Representatives, as well as for many state and local representative positions. In a representative democracy such as ours, one way that people exercise their authority is by voting in elections. Voting allows citizens, once they have reached the age of 18, the opportunity to have their voices heard and to influence the government. They decide whom they want to represent them, and sometimes at elections, they vote on certain issues. With their vote, they can also remove officials who ignore their intentions or who betray their trust.

Once we have elected our representatives, we must still be careful to limit their power, and one way we do this is through a system of checks and balances.

A Minute with Senator WordSmart

Set # 3

Take a minute to review the meanings of some new words by matching the word or phrase with its definition.

1. Majority rule

2. Minority

3. Freedom of speech

4. Popular sovereignty

5. Candidate

6. Election

7. Vote

a. To select a candidate or decide on an issue in an election.

b. The right to question and criticize the policies and actions of our elected officials.

c. A group with less people in it than the majority.

d. The source of government's authority is in the people.

e. To rule by the choice of the majority (more than half) who vote on something.

f. A process by which people vote for their leaders.

g. An individual wishing to be representative of the people.

By using a framework of representation, checks and balances, and federalism (the division of political power between the national government and the individual state governments), we have achieved a government that is powerful enough to keep order in the country, defend us from foreign threats, and provide various services, while at the same time not interfering with our basic rights and freedoms.

Surf's up...

Check out this site to learn more about constitutional democracies:

pbs.org/weta/forcemorepowerful/classroom/lesson1/corevalues.html

The Choice Is Yours
Set # 2

To check your understanding of the previous material, answer the following questions by selecting the letter of the correct answer.

1. The branches of our government are _____.
   a. legislative and judicial
   b. presidential and legislative
   c. state and national
   d. judicial, legislative, and executive

2. Federalism divides political power between the national government and the _____.
   a. president
   b. state governments
   c. judicial branch
   d. Congress

3. The following is an example of a check and balance in our system of government:
   a. the president vetoing a bill that Congress passed.
   b. the Supreme Court disallowing a law because it conflicts with the Constitution.
   c. Congress amending the Constitution.
   d. all of the above.

4. Because we select our representatives and decide issues by majority rule, it is important to _____ in order to preserve our ideals about government.
   a. be popular
   b. protect the rights of the minority
   c. try to be part of the majority
   d. spend a lot of money during the election

5. We select our representatives by:
   a. pulling their name out of the president's hat.
   b. determining who has the most education.
   c. asking the Supreme Court.
   d. voting for them in elections.

Projects You Can Do

Use the Internet or your local public library to:

1. Read about the ancient Greek system of direct democracy. Who participated in this system of government? What were some of its advantages, and some of its disadvantages?
2. Learn about how the founders of our country came up with their ideas on representation, checks and balances, and federalism.
3. Identify the similarities and differences between our system of government and that of another country, such as Great Britain or Brazil.

Now that we understand our system of government, let's find out how it was built. Let's look at our constitutional foundation.

CHAPTER TWO

Our Constitutional Foundation

THE PATH TO DEMOCRACY

By the mid-1700s, Great Britain controlled an area of North America that stretched from the Atlantic Coast, west to the Appalachian Mountains, and from what is now Maine to the northern border of Florida. This land was home to close to one million Europeans, a quarter-million Africans, and a quarter-million Native Americans. Although settlers had been arriving in British North America since the 1600s, their numbers swelled in the 1700s. Because of this rapid growth, along with the diversity of settlers and geographic differences, British North America was developing a character of its own, much different from Britain.

Historians divide British North America into three distinct regions: the New England colonies, the Mid-Atlantic colonies, and the southern colonies. The colonies of Massachusetts, Connecticut, Rhode Island, and New Hampshire comprised the *New England colonies*. Seeking freedom from religious perse-cution, English Puritans started settling the New England region in the early 1600s. A century later, the descendants of these first settlers formed the overwhelming majority of the population, making the New England colonies the most culturally and religiously homogenous (alike) of the three colonial regions. Because of its cold climate and rocky soils, New England couldn't cultivate large farms, so it took advantage of its Atlantic coastline and developed a large shipping industry.

A different society developed in the ***Mid-Atlantic colonies*** of Pennsylvania, Delaware, New York, and New Jersey. Immigrants from England and Wales, who were members of the religious Society of Friends (more commonly known as Quakers), initially settled in Pennsylvania, Delaware, and parts of New Jersey. At the same time, Dutch immigrants settled throughout New York and formed a majority of the state's population until the beginning of the 1700s, much the same as the Puritans controlled New England. However, beginning in the early 1700s, tens of thousands of Germans and Scots, as well as large numbers of Irish people, immigrated to the Mid-Atlantic colonies. Within 50 years, the Mid-Atlantic colonies were a mixture of languages and cultures—a contrast to the New England colonies to the north. They were also a contrast economically; the Mid-Atlantic settlers were farmers who took advantage of the region's fertile soil to grow crops for export to Europe.

English settlers, much different from the New England and Mid-Atlantic settlers, occupied the ***southern colonies***, which included Virginia, Maryland, North Carolina, South Carolina, and Georgia. These settlers, most of whom were quite wealthy, came to North America seeking greater wealth. The region's mild climate permitted them to establish large plantations to produce tobacco and rice for export to European markets. At first, the wealthy planters imported English indentured servants who worked the planters' lands for a specified period in return for their passage to America. However, by the late 1600s, plantation owners increasingly turned to slave labor from Africa, and by the mid-1700s, they had imported so many Africans that the southern colonies had become slave societies, sharply divided along the lines of race and economic class.

The result? In the mid-1700s, there wasn't one "American" colonial society, but three regional societies with little in common except their political ties to the British Empire. As time passed, however, all came to believe in *self-rule*—that is, the citizens should govern themselves, not be governed by an outside power. Nevertheless, it was hard for these different regions to agree on how to attain this goal.

The Choice Is Yours
Set # 1

To check your understanding of the previous material, answer the following questions by selecting the letter of the correct answer. If you want to check your work, refer to the Answer Key in the back of the book.

1. British North America was composed of _____ distinct geographic areas and cultures.
   a. two
   b. three
   c. four
   d. five

2. Which of the following graphs best shows the relationship of the number of Europeans to the number of Native Americans in the mid-1700s in British North America?

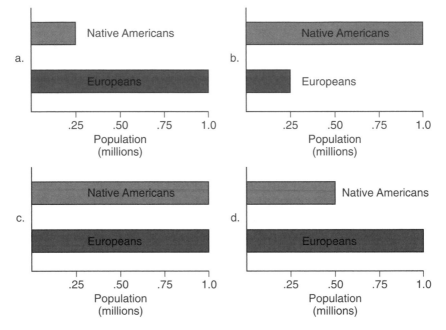

3. Into which region of British North America did the Puritans settle?
   a. The southern colonies
   b. The New England colonies
   c. The Mid-Atlantic colonies
   d. The Puritans didn't settle in British North America

4. The _____ colonies were the most culturally diverse.
   a. Mid-Atlantic
   b. southern
   c. New England
   d. Quaker

5. At first, wealthy southern planters imported _____ to work on the tobacco and rice plantations.
   a. Africans
   b. Native Americans
   c. Asians
   d. indentured Europeans

THE DECLARATION OF INDEPENDENCE TO THE CONSTITUTION

Eventually, each of the three regions suffered under the harsh rule of the British. The British heavily taxed the commerce of the New England merchants, hurting their shipping business. The farmers of the Mid-Atlantic colonies were saddled with high taxes and unfair pricing of their goods. British markets kept the price unreasonably low for sugar and cotton produced by the plantation owners in the southern colonies. As a result, the different regions eventually united to fight the abuses of a common enemy. Unfortunately, King George III refused to listen to the pleas of the Colonists, causing increased discontentedness among them. As this discontentedness grew stronger during the 1770s, the talk of revolution to achieve self-rule also became stronger. Fighting between Colonists and British soldiers occurred more frequently over the next two years as the Colonists continued to cut their ties with Britain. Nevertheless, in spite of all this, the Colonists continued trying to compromise with King George.

When the *Second Continental Congress* first met in May 1775, the king still had not replied to the list of grievances that the First Continental Congress had sent him. Consequently, the Congress gradually assumed the responsibilities of a national government. In June 1775, the Congress established the Continental Army, as well as a continental currency and a postal system for the "United Colonies."

A Minute with Senator WordSmart
Set # 1

Take a minute to make sure that you understand the meanings of the new words. Match the word in the left-hand column with its definition in the right-hand column by drawing a line from the word to its definition. If you want to check your work, review the Answer Key in the back of the book.

1. New England colonies

    a. The group who assumed the responsibility to act as the national government for the colonists.

2. Mid-Atlantic colonies

    b. Virginia, Maryland, North Carolina, South Carolina, and Georgia.

3. Southern colonies

    c. The concept that citizens should govern themselves, not be governed by some outside power.

4. Self-rule

    d. Pennsylvania, Delaware, New York, and New Jersey.

5. Second Continental Congress

    e. Massachusetts, Connecticut, Rhode Island, and New Hampshire.

By mid-1776, the Second Continental Congress had lost patience with King George, so representatives appointed the *Committee of Five* to present the colonies' reasons for desiring independence from British rule. The Committee of Five had representatives from each of the three regions. John Adams of Massachusetts and Roger Sherman of Connecticut represented the New England colonies; Benjamin Franklin of Pennsylvania and Robert Livingston of New York represented the Mid-Atlantic colonies; and Thomas Jefferson of Virginia alone represented the southern colonies.

Jefferson, with the help of Franklin and Adams, drafted a proclamation that the Colonists would send to the king. After a few minor changes, Congress adopted the *Declaration of Independence* on July 4, 1776.

The Declaration of Independence, which you will find in the Appendix, contains five parts:

- the Introduction
- the Preamble
- the First Section of the Body
- the Second Section of the Body
- the Conclusion.

The Introduction "declares" the reasons why the colonies need to be independent from the British Empire. Next, the Preamble explains views about freedom and self-rule now common to the three regions. The First Section of the Body states the abuses of King George III, and the Second Section explains how the Colonists appealed in vain to the king, concluding that the United Colonies have the right to be free from the tyrant.

Surf's up...

The Declaration of Independence is one of our country's treasures. To learn more about the history of this important document, take a look at this site:

archives.gov/exhibit_hall/charters_of_freedom/
declaration/declaration_history.html

Did You Know?

John Hancock, the president of the Second Continental Congress, was the first to sign the Declaration of Independence, which was written on a sheet of parchment measuring $24\frac{1}{4}$ inches by $29\frac{3}{4}$ inches. Hancock centered his bold signature below the text. As was their custom, the other delegates signed at the right, below the text, their signatures arranged according to the geographic location of the states they represented. New Hampshire, the northernmost state, began the list; Georgia, the southernmost, ended it.

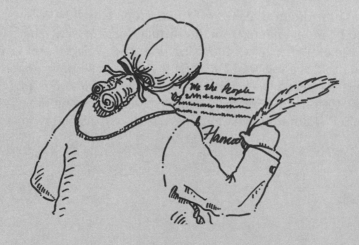

Things to Think About

1. The three regions of colonies were so culturally and economically different. What were some of the concerns the colonists in each region would have had?
2. After you have read the Declaration of Independence, discuss some of the reasons why the colonists were upset with King George III.

Articles of Confederation: a step toward the Constitution

The Declaration of Independence did just that—it declared our independence. However, once the colonies had made the break from Britain and war broke out, they needed written laws and a more detailed framework for the new government. In 1777, during the Revolutionary War, the Continental Congress wrote the *Articles of Confederation*, a national governing code to provide the colonies with a unified government as they fought for their independence. The head of the committee, John Dickinson, presented their work to the Congress on July 12, 1776, eight days after the signing of the Declaration of Independence. Dickinson initially proposed a strong *central government*—that is, a national government that governs from one "central" location. However, because of their experience with Great Britain, the Congressional representatives feared a powerful central government; consequently, after much discussion, they changed Dickinson's proposed articles drastically before they sent them to all states for *ratification*, or approval, in November 1777.

The Continental Congress had been careful to give the states as much power and independence as possible and to limit the functions and powers of the national government. Even with these limits, it took until March 1781 for all 13 states to ratify the Articles of Confederation.

The Articles of Confederation are in the Appendix. As you read them, you will notice they created a "league of friendship" among the states, rather than a centralized national government. As a result, the new government wasn't strong enough to deal

LEAGUE OF FRIENDSHIP

with the problems facing the fledgling nation. Consequently, each state began to act alone in its own best interest; before long, the new nation was disintegrating. A new centralized government was needed to help the states work together as a unified nation.

To accomplish that task, in May 1787, the ***Constitutional Convention*** was held in Philadelphia, Pennsylvania. Delegates from every state except Rhode Island, which refused to send a delegate because it was afraid of losing its rights as a sovereign state, met to try to save the new nation. Once together, they worked for four months drafting a document that would create a new government.

A Minute with Senator WordSmart
Set # 2

Take a minute to make sure that you understand the meanings of the new words by matching the word or phrase with its definition.

1. Committee of Five

a. The first national governing code of the United States; it was drafted in 1777, ratified in 1781, and replaced by the present Constitution.

2. Declaration of Independence

   b. The group appointed to present the colonies' reasons for desiring independence from British rule.

3. Articles of Confederation

   c. The document written chiefly by Thomas Jefferson and adopted on July 4, 1776, by the Second Continental Congress that stated the reasons the colonies needed to break away from British rule.

4. Central government

   d. Approval.

5. Ratification

   e. The meeting in Philadelphia from May 25 through September 17, 1787, during which the delegates worked to replace the government of the Articles of Confederation with a strong central government.

6. Constitutional Convention

   f. A form of government in which the national government governs from one "central" location.

The Constitution

After all their hard work, the question was, Would the states ratify the new document created at the convention—the *Constitution of the United States*? It would provide a framework for a new government different from the current "league of friendship." To many people, it might seem like a return to how it was under British rule. After all, the Colonists had fought a war to rid themselves of a strong central government that took away their personal liberties and oppressed them with heavy taxes.

The delegates pressed on, and by the end of 1787, Delaware, Pennsylvania, and New Jersey had approved the framework for a new government. The delegates had decided that the Constitution would become the law of the land and would establish the new government as soon as nine of the thirteen states approved it. Would six other states ratify the Constitution? The government the Articles of Confederation created wasn't working, but would the people feel that the government the Constitution created would be better?

Many thought it would, but others felt differently. Those who favored the Constitution, and thus a strong central government, were known as *Federalists*. On the other hand, the *Anti-Federalists* believed that the Constitution created an unnecessarily strong national government, leaving the states and the people with too little power.

The Federalists and the Anti-Federalists argued in the press, the legislatures, and the state conventions. Alexander Hamilton, James Madison, and John Jay spoke in favor of the Constitution, and their arguments helped persuade the citizens of Massachusetts and New York to ratify the Constitution. At the same time, George Washington was working hard to convince his fellow Virginians. However, by the time Virginia finally accepted the Constitution, nine states had given their approval; the new government had been approved. Nevertheless, the support of Washington's state was considered an important vote of confidence for the new government.

Did You Know?

On June 21, 1788, New Hampshire became the ninth state to ratify the Constitution, making it the law of the land.

Surf's up...

Want to learn more about the Articles of Confederation?

Check out this site:

   congressforkids.net/articlesofconfederation.htm

Here's one that takes you through how the Constitution was written:

   congressforkids.net/writingconstitution.htm

The Constitution has become the world's oldest charter of national government in continuous use. With just 27 *amendments* (additions), it continues to provide the road map for our government. (Chapter Three discusses some of the more important amendments.) The Constitutional Convention delegates recognized the United States as a government of the people, not of the states. Consequently, the Constitution embodies the principle that out of many different peoples, one national society can be created.

Projects You Can Do

1. Use the Internet or your local public library to learn about a seventeenth century philosopher named John Locke. How did his views shape Jefferson's writing of the Declaration of Independence?
2. The Articles of Confederation and the Constitution are in the Appendix. Compare the documents. How are they different? How are they similar?
3. Use the Internet or your local public library to learn more about the Federalists and the Anti-Federalists. Why did these groups disagree? What did each group favor, and why? Why did the Federalists end up getting their way?

As we have seen, the authors of the Constitution wanted a strong central government, but they knew from experience that a strong central government could become harsh and unfair. Consequently, the Constitution would need ways to keep the new government from becoming too strong. They accomplished this through a system of *checks and balances*, which, as mentioned previously, refers to the ways each branch of our government limits the power of the branches, or parts.

One of these checks and balances is the *separation of powers*. Rather than one body in the government having all the power, the Constitution divides, or separates, the power among the branches of the government.

THE SEPARATION OF POWERS

To implement this separation of powers, the authors of the Constitution established three branches of government, using the first three *articles* or major divisions of the Constitution:

- Article I establishes the **legislative branch**, which is the *lawmaking* part of the government. The U.S. Congress comprises the legislative branch. (See Chapter Four to learn more about the legislative branch.)

☆ LEGISLATIVE BRANCH ☆

- Article II establishes the **executive branch**, which is the *law-enforcing* part of the government. The executive branch includes the president and the vice president. (Chapter Five discusses the executive branch.)

- Article III establishes the *judicial branch*, which is the *law-interpreting* part of the government. The judicial branch includes the Supreme Court and lower federal courts. (See Chapter Six for more information about the judicial branch.)

A Minute with Senator WordSmart
Set # 3

Take a minute to make sure that you understand the meanings of the new words by matching the word or phrase with its definition.

1. Federalists

2. Anti-Federalists

3. Constitution of the United States

4. Amendment

5. Checks and balances

6. Separation of powers

7. Legislative branch

8. Executive branch

9. Judicial branch

a. An addition.

b. A document setting out the laws that are the framework for our nation.

c. The lawmaking part of the government, which includes Congress.

d. They preferred a strong central government.

e. The law-enforcing part of our government, which includes the president and vice president.

f. They preferred a weak central government and strong state governments.

g. The law-interpreting part of our government, which includes the Supreme Court and other federal courts.

h. The ways each branch of government limits the power of the other branches.

i. The governing power is divided, or separated, among branches of the government.

CITIZENS AND THE NEW GOVERNMENT

The remaining four articles of the Constitution address important matters regarding the relationship between the people and the new government.

- Article IV begins with the *Full Faith and Credit Clause*, which says that each state shall respect the laws of the other states. It then establishes the process for admitting new states and, finally, guarantees a republican—or representative—form of government for all states.
- Article V establishes procedures for amending or adding to the Constitution.

- Article VI establishes that the Constitution and the laws of the United States are the "supreme Law of the Land." We refer to this as the *supremacy article*.
- Article VII states that ratification or approval of the Constitution by nine states would be sufficient to adopt the Constitution. Eventually, all states ratified the document.

Things to Think About

1. Article V establishes the requirements for amending the Constitution. Notice how difficult it is to amend the Constitution. Why?
2. Why did the writers of the Constitution include Article VI, the supremacy article?

The Choice Is Yours
Set # 2

To check your understanding of the previous material, answer the following questions by selecting the letter of the correct answer.

1. The following is the correct order in which the documents were ratified:
   a. Constitution, Declaration of Independence, Articles of Confederation
   b. Declaration of Independence, Constitution, Articles of Confederation
   c. Articles of Confederation, Declaration of Independence, Constitution
   d. Declaration of Independence, Articles of Confederation, Constitution

2. Article II of the Constitution establishes the _____ branch(es) of our government.
   a. judicial
   b. executive
   c. legislative
   d. judicial, executive, and legislative

3. The Constitution establishes _____ branch(es) of government.
   a. three
   b. two
   c. one
   d. four

4. The portion of the Constitution that requires each state to respect the laws of the other states is the _____.
   a. Supremacy article
   b. Preamble
   c. Legislative article
   d. Full Faith and Credit Clause

5. The Constitutional Convention was held in _____ in 1787.
   a. New York City
   b. Washington, D.C.
   c. Annapolis
   d. Philadelphia

FEDERALISM

Along with the separation of powers, federalism is another check and balance established in the Constitution that keeps the national government from becoming too powerful. *Federalism* is a way of organizing government so that the power is divided between the national government and other governmental bodies, such as state governments. Because this method to check and balance power assigns each government its own powers, we also call this *dual sovereignty*.

The Constitution specifically grants certain powers to the national government, such as declaring war, negotiating treaties, and raising armies. Consequently, it denies the states powers granted to the national government because if the states were allowed to engage in these actions, it would weaken or undermine the national government. However, the boundary between national and state powers and responsibilities is sometimes unclear because the state and national government cooperate in areas ranging from public assistance for the poor to transportation, and because they serve the same people.

STATE AND LOCAL GOVERNMENTS

In our federal system, the national government may exercise only those powers that the Constitution grants to it. All other powers belong to the state governments. The *state government* is the central government for the state and is located in that state's capital city. State governments plan and pay for most roads in the state, run public schools, provide water, establish zoning regulations, license professions, and arrange elections for their state's citizens. Although the national government is far larger today than in the early days of the Constitution, the state governments have grown even more. In fact, over the past decades, each state's power, especially over social services, has rapidly expanded.

Just as the boundary of responsibility between the national and state governments isn't always precise, the same is true with state and *local governments*, which are city (municipal), township, and county governments. Local governments provide police and fire services, as well as basic human services, such as garbage collection. However, because local authority comes from specific state constitutional provisions or from laws passed by state legislatures, the state has the final decision over local functions, such as police forces and fire departments.

Did You Know?

Although there are only 50 state governments, there are more than 40,000 county, municipal, and township governments.

Surf's up...

State and local governments take care of many important jobs. To learn more about everything they do, check out these sites:

statelocalgov.net/
loc.gov/global/state/

A Minute with Senator WordSmart
Set # 4

Take a minute to make sure that you understand the meanings of the new words by matching the word or phrase with its definition.

1. Full Faith and Credit Clause
2. Supremacy article

3. Federalism
4. Dual sovereignty

5. State government

6. Local government

a. A county, municipal, or township government.
b. The central government for a state.
c. Article VI of the Constitution.
d. The beginning of Article IV, which says that each state shall respect the laws of the other states.
e. Refers to a type of government in which the power is divided between the national government and other governmental units.
f. Another name for federalism.

Projects You Can Do

1. Use the Internet or your local public library to learn more about the concerns mentioned by the Anti-Federalists. Are their concerns still valid today?
2. Find out which offices of the federal or national government are located in your city. What functions do they perform? Find out which offices of the state government are located in your city. What functions do they perform?
3. Learn about your city government. Who is your mayor? Who are the members of your city council? What are some of the issues facing your city's government?

We've learned about the constitutional foundation for our national, as well as, state and local government. We've also learned about the checks and balances on the power of the government. Next, let's see how we have continued to protect our individual rights and liberties.

CHAPTER THREE

Civil Liberties and Civil Rights

CIVIL LIBERTIES AND THE CONSTITUTION

Many of the delegates ratified the Constitution on the condition that the Congress promise to do more to protect the civil liberties of the people from possible abuses by the newly formed government. *Civil liberties* are the individual freedoms and rights we expect as citizens. Consequently, in September 1789, soon after the Continental Congress ratified the Constitution, Congress proposed 12 *amendments* (additions) to the document, ten of which were approved in December 1791, creating the *Bill of Rights*.

Many of the congressional delegates didn't believe that additional protection of civil liberties was necessary because the Constitution already guaranteed citizens several liberties. For example,

- You are liberated from cruel kings because the Constitution forbids anyone from taking a title of nobility. [Article I, Section 9]
- If you are accused of a crime, you are guaranteed a trial by *jury* (a group of citizens who will decide your guilt or innocence). [Article III, Section 2]
- If you travel to another state, you are protected by that state's laws, as if you lived in that state. [Article IV, Section 2]
- The police are not allowed to keep you in jail unless you have been charged with a crime. Your liberty is protected through a writ of habeas corpus. *Habeas corpus* translated means, "produce the body." A *writ of habeas corpus* is a court order directing police to bring you into court and explain to the judge why you are in jail. If a judge determines that you are being jailed unlawfully, the judge must order your immediate release. [Article I, Section 9]
- Congress is prohibited from passing a *bill of attainder*, which is any law that punishes, without trial, individuals belonging to a group singled out by the government. [Article I, Section 9]
- Congress may not pass *ex post facto laws*, which are laws making something you did a crime that wasn't a crime when you did it or increasing the punishment for a crime after the crime was committed. [Article I, Section 9]

- The Constitution limits who can be punished for **treason** (the crime of betraying your country) to the person committing the treason, which means that family and friends may not also be punished. [Article III, Section 3]
- Each state must establish and maintain a **republican form of government**—that is, a representative form of government. [Article IV, Section 4]
- You can't be prohibited from serving in a public office because of your religious beliefs. [Article VI]

A Minute with Senator WordSmart
Set # 1

Take a minute to make sure that you understand the meanings of the new words. Match the word in the left-hand column with its definition in the right-hand column by drawing a line from the word to its definition. If you want to check your work, review the Answer Key in the back of the book.

1. Civil liberties
2. Bill of Rights
3. Amendment

4. Writ of habeas corpus

5. Bill of attainder

6. Ex post facto law

7. Treason

8. Republican form of government

a. Representative government.
b. An addition.
c. A law that now punishes a person for doing something that was legal at the time the person did it.
d. A written demand to the police to explain to a judge why they have imprisoned someone.
e. The crime of betraying your country.
f. The first ten amendments to the Constitution.
g. The individual freedoms and rights we expect as citizens.
h. A law that punishes individuals in a group without a trial.

The Choice Is Yours
Set # 1

You will find a copy of the Constitution in the Appendix. Use it to find where the following civil liberties are located. Select the letter of the correct answer. If you want to check your work, refer to the Answer Key in the back of the book.

1. This part forbids the granting of titles of nobility, as well as bills of attainder and ex post facto laws. Also, it guarantees liberty through the writ of habeas corpus.
   a. Article I, Section 9
   b. Article II
   c. Article VI
   d. Article III, Section 3

2. This part protects people traveling from one state to another state.
   a. Article I, Section 9
   b. Article VI
   c. Article III, Section 3
   d. Article IV, Section 2

3. This part guarantees a person accused of a crime a trial by jury.
   a. Article IV, Section 2
   b. Article VI
   c. Article III, Section 2
   d. Article I, Section 9

4. This part limits the punishment for treason to the person committing the crime.
   a. Article IV, Section 1
   b. Article III, Section 3
   c. Article VI
   d. Article II, Section 1

5. This part requires the states to have representative governments.
   a. Article IV, Section 2
   b. Article III, Section 3
   c. Article II
   d. Article IV, Section 4

6. This part prohibits a person from not being able to hold a public office because of that person's religious beliefs.
   a. Article II
   b. Article I
   c. Article VII
   d. Article VI

Things to Think About

1. Why is the writ of habeas corpus important to our personal liberty?
2. How does the requirement that a person accused of a crime is entitled to a trial by jury create an important personal liberty?

BILL OF RIGHTS

The Bill of Rights is in the Appendix. These are the first ten amendments to the Constitution. Refer to the following summary as you look over the amendments:

The ***First Amendment*** guarantees several liberties, including freedom of religion, freedom of speech, freedom of press, and freedom of assembly (the freedom to get together and discuss things).

Freedom of religion

Unlike many countries, the United States doesn't have an official or state religion. The first two clauses of the First Amendment guarantee us religious liberty:

> Congress shall make no law respecting an establishment of religion [Establishment Clause], or prohibiting [preventing] the free exercise thereof [Free Exercise Clause].

On writing what has come to be called the **Establishment Clause**, the delegates were reacting to the English system, in which the king or queen was the head, not only of the government but also of the church established by the government—the Church of England. Consequently, public officials were required to swear an oath of support for the Church of England as a condition of holding office. However, the Establishment Clause goes beyond merely forbidding the establishment of a national religion; it is designed to prevent the government from:

- sponsoring or favoring any religion
- supporting a religious group
- involving itself in religious matters.

The **Free Exercise Clause** guarantees our liberty to practice religion without interference from the government. The delegates knew that many of the people they were representing had come to America to escape religious persecution.

Freedom of speech, press, and assembly

The First Amendment also prohibits the government from interfering with our liberties of freedom of speech, freedom of the press, and freedom of assembly, which is our right to "peaceably assemble." Consequently, it is probably the most important amendment in the Bill of Rights. Free speech isn't simply the personal liberty or freedom of individuals to speak their minds; it is also the liberty for the rest of us to hear what they have to say. For example, if a person doesn't like something the government is doing, it is important for us to hear the reasons for that position; after all, we might find out that we don't like the action either. Our government representatives are more likely to listen to many voices, than just one. Furthermore, to have an effective democracy, we as voters must be allowed to hear the views of the candidates running for office so that we can choose the people who will best represent us.

Did You Know?

The Supreme Court ruled in 1919 that freedom of speech could be restricted if the words could endanger people. For example, it is against the law to shout "Fire!" in a crowded theater that isn't on fire.

The **Second Amendment** guarantees the liberty to keep and bear arms (guns) as part of a **state militia**—citizens who have been trained so that they can be called on in a time of military emergency, although they aren't part of the regular armed forces. Today's state militia is the National Guard.

The **Third Amendment** prohibits the stationing of troops in homes without consent. This isn't a problem today, but it was in the late 1700s when the Colonists were forced to allow British soldiers to live in their homes.

Things to Think About

1. Think of some situations where the rights of free speech and assembly would be important. Should there be limits on these rights?
2. Read the Second Amendment. Why was it important for the Colonists to have the liberty to own firearms so that they could serve in their state's militia? Does this reason still exist today?

The civil liberties of people accused of crimes are protected by the Fourth, Fifth, and Sixth Amendments. The *Fourth Amendment* protects against improper searches by the police by requiring the police to have a search warrant. A judge will issue a *search warrant* to search a particular place or person only after the police convince that person that they have a good reason for wanting to search. If the police conduct a search without a warrant, the evidence gathered can't be used against the person in court.

Did You Know?

Despite what we sometimes see on television, outside of some special circumstances, police officers aren't allowed to break down doors and invade homes. A police search without a warrant is unconstitutional.

The *Fifth Amendment* protects a person accused of a serious crime in a number of ways:

- It requires that a grand jury review the accusations or charges. A *grand jury* is a special group of citizens who investigate accusations against persons charged with a serious crime to determine if enough evidence exists to bring charges against the accused person.

- It prohibits **double jeopardy** (being tried twice for the same crime).
- It prohibits **self-incrimination**, which means individuals can't be forced to testify against themselves. During the seventeenth century, the English forced confessions from religious dissenters. Because the colonial congressmen were familiar with this practice, they did not allow the government to force people to testify against themselves in criminal prosecutions.

- The amendment's **Due Process Clause** states that "no person shall be deprived of life, liberty, or property without due process of law." **Due process of law** is agreed-upon rules and procedures that keep those in government from creating their own rules and procedures, possibly abusing their power.

Did You Know?

An important aspect of due process of law in recent decades has been its expansion to protect our right to privacy. Although there is no mention of privacy in the Constitution, we have recognized that certain parts of the First, Fourth, Fifth, Ninth, and Fourteenth Amendments apply to our personal privacy.

A Minute with Senator WordSmart
Set # 2

Take a minute to make sure that you understand the meanings of the new words by matching the word or phrase with its definition.

1. Establishment Clause of the First Amendment

2. Free Exercise Clause of the First Amendment

3. State militia

4. Search warrant

5. Grand jury

6. Double jeopardy

7. Self-incrimination

8. Due Process Clause of the Fifth Amendment

9. Due process of law

a. Testifying against yourself in court.

b. The accepted rules and regulations that keep those in government from abusing their power.

c. A document issued by a judge that authorizes the police to search a particular place or person.

d. It prohibits Congress from establishing an official religion.

e. No person shall be deprived of life, liberty, or property without due process of law.

f. It allows us to practice our religion without interference from the government.

g. To be tried twice for the same crime.

h. A special group of citizens who investigate accusations against persons to determine if enough evidence exists to bring charges.

i. Citizens who serve in time of military emergency although they aren't part of the regular armed forces.

A *criminal offense* is one in which an individual is charged with committing a crime of violating a law that protects another person's safety. The punishment is usually imprisonment (jail). According to the *Sixth Amendment*, an individual charged with a criminal offense is guaranteed the right to:

- have a speedy trial by an impartial(fair) jury,
- be informed of the charges made against the person, and
- have legal representation.

The *Seventh Amendment* guarantees a trial by jury in most civil law disputes. *Civil law disputes* are disputes among individual citizens or among individual citizens and government officials over property or money (a "fine"). Unlike criminal offenses, the punishment is usually paying money, not going to jail.

For people charged with a crime, the *Eighth Amendment* guarantees the liberty of freedom until proven guilty by prohibiting excessive bail. (*Bail* is money deposited with the court that temporarily releases a person from jail.

Get Out of Jail

Bail Isn't Free

Did You Know?

Over the years, many people have argued that the death penalty is "cruel and unusual punishment." However, so far, Congress has left the decision of whether to continue executing individuals convicted of certain crimes to each state.

The person "posting" the bail assures that the released person will appear at trial.)

Also, if a person is convicted of a crime, the Eighth Amendment prohibits the government from punishing that person with excessive fines or with any cruel and unusual punishment.

The *Ninth Amendment* assures that the government doesn't deny people liberties or rights not specifically mentioned in the Constitution. These are referred to as *implied* liberties or rights; that is, not all liberties and rights are mentioned in the Constitution, but the creators wanted the people to have them, nonetheless.

The **Tenth Amendment** gives to the states or the people powers not granted to Congress or denied to the states. This keeps the national government from taking more power, possibly interfering with the liberties of the citizens.

Surf's up...

The liberties guaranteed by the Bill of Rights are important to us all. These two sites will help you learn more about the Bill of Rights and its history:

earlyamerica.com/earlyamerica/freedom/bill/index. html
rain.org/~karpeles/billrightsdisc.html

The Choice Is Yours
Set # 2

To check your understanding of the previous material, answer the following questions by selecting the letter of the correct answer.

1. The _____ Amendment guarantees a person accused of a crime the right to a speedy trial.
   a. First
   b. Third
   c. Fifth
   d. Sixth

2. The rights of people accused of crimes are protected by the
   _____ Amendment(s).
   a. Fourth
   b. Fifth
   c. Sixth
   d. Fourth, Fifth, and Sixth

3. Freedom to practice your religion is guaranteed by the _____
   Amendment.
   a. First
   b. Second
   c. Fifth
   d. Tenth

4. The right to get together to discuss the government is referred
   to as _____.
   a. freedom of religion
   b. freedom to vote
   c. freedom of assembly
   d. freedom of press

5. Powers not given to Congress or denied to the states are
   given to the people or the states by the _____ Amendment.
   a. First
   b. Tenth
   c. Sixth
   d. Fourth

CIVIL LIBERTIES AND THE STATES

By design, the Bill of Rights applies only to the national government, not state governments. Why doesn't it apply to the states? The writers who proposed the Bill of Rights were confident that states could control their own state officials; also, most state constitutions already had bills of rights. Unfortunately, over time, it became apparent that enforcement of the protections varied widely.

To deal with this situation, the Fourteenth Amendment was adopted in 1868. In Section 1 of this amendment are its *Due Process Clause* and the *Equal Protection Clause*:

> No State shall make or enforce any law which shall abridge the privileges or immunities of citizens of the United States; nor shall any State deprive any person of life, liberty, or property, without due process of law [Due Process Clause]; nor deny to any person within its jurisdiction the equal protection of the laws [Equal Protection Clause].

If you go back and read the Fifth Amendment, you will see that its Due Process Clause assures that the *national government* doesn't deprive people of life, liberty, or property without due process of law. By comparison, the Due Process Clause and the Equal Protection Clause of the Fourteenth Amendment protect our civil liberties from possible abuses by state governments.

Surf's up...

Check out this site for more history and explanation regarding the Fourteenth Amendment:

caselaw.lp.findlaw.com/data/constitution/amendment14/

A Minute with Senator WordSmart
Set # 3

Take a minute to make sure that you understand the meanings of the new words by matching the word or phrase with its definition.

1. Criminal offense

2. Civil law disputes

3. Bail

4. Due Process Clause of the Fourteenth Amendment

5. Equal Protection Clause of the Fourteenth Amendment

a. The money deposited with the court that releases a person temporarily from jail on the assurance that the person will appear at the trial.

b. No state shall deny to any person within its jurisdiction equal protection of the laws.

c. The government charges an individual with committing a crime because he or she violated a law that protects another person's safety.

d. A dispute between individual citizens or individual citizens and government officials over property or money.

e. No person shall be deprived of life, liberty, or property without due process of law; extends the liberties and protections of the Bill of Rights to individual residents of states.

CIVIL RIGHTS

Many people confuse the terms *civil liberties* and *civil rights*. As we have seen, civil liberties are certain individual freedoms and rights that we expect as citizens, and the Bill of Rights and the Fourteenth Amendment protect these freedoms and rights for us from possible government abuses. These liberties include freedom of religion, speech, and press, along with the rights and liberties guaranteed to people accused of crimes.

Civil rights, on the other hand, are the rights of citizens not to be discriminated against because of their race, sex, or disability. As opposed to civil liberties, which are ours to protect us from the government, civil rights are what we expect the government to provide to every individual. Civil rights include the right to vote, equality in job opportunities, and equal access to housing and education. Selected constitutional amendments, following the Bill of Rights, address these rights.

Since the enactment of the Bill of Rights, we have amended the Constitution only 17 times in more than 200 years. Although numerous amendments have been proposed in Congress, only a fraction of them have gone to the states for approval. Of the amendments approved, several have addressed civil rights:

Amendment	Year Adopted	Accomplished
Thirteenth	1865	Abolished slavery.
Fourteenth	1868	Due process and equal protection of the laws guaranteed in the states.
Fifteenth	1870	Gave African-Americans the right to vote.
Nineteenth	1920	Gave women the right to vote.
Twenty-Sixth	1971	Lowered the minimum voting age from 21 years to 18 years.

Civil rights of minorities

The Thirteenth Amendment abolished slavery, and the Fifteenth Amendment gave African-Americans the right to vote. Unfortunately, practices such as discrimination and segregation persisted long after these amendments were ratified.

Through the efforts of civil rights workers, the Supreme Court, and various legislators, the civil rights of minorities have become more well established. The Civil Rights Act of 1964 ended segregation of schools and public facilities and required equal opportunities for employment. To enforce these rights, the legislation gave the executive branch of the government the power to discontinue federal financial aid to local and state governments that discriminated based on race. This provided an incentive for the states to desegregate relatively quickly. Shortly thereafter, the Voting Rights Act of 1965 eliminated most barriers to voting.

It is important to remember that the Equal Protection Clause of the Fifth Amendment and of the Fourteenth Amendment apply only to the action of governments, not to that of private individuals. If an individual performs a discriminatory action, it doesn't violate the Constitution; however, it may violate federal and state laws.

Civil rights of women

In 1900, four states—Colorado, Idaho, Utah, and Wyoming—granted women the right to vote in state and local elections. Yet, it wasn't until 1919, with the ratification of the Nineteenth Amendment, that women everywhere were allowed to vote in all elections. Voting, however, is only one civil right of concern for women. As more and more women enter the workforce, they demand equal rights to jobs and pay, and women have made much progress in this area. Most recently, however, the proposed equal rights amendment, which would have been our twenty-eighth amendment, failed to win enough support, suggesting that Congress and state legislatures still have work to do.

Civil rights of the disabled

Physical barriers and discrimination have prevented the disabled from enjoying many of the benefits of being citizens. The Due Process and Equal Protection Clauses of the Fifth and the Fourteenth Amendments, respectively, were inadequate; in part, because they applied only to national and state governments, not private companies and individuals. Consequently, in 1990, Congress passed the Americans with Disabilities Act, which made it against the law to discriminate against the disabled, including in employment, transportation, and public accommodations.

Surf's up...

The struggle for civil rights is an important part of our history. The following site provides a lot of information on various civil rights:

usdoj.gov/kidspage/crt/crtmenu.htm

Civil rights of the young and the aged

Within the past five years, Congress has passed legislation protecting the rights of older Americans, especially their right to employment. For citizens on the other end of the age spectrum, the Twenty-Sixth Amendment was ratified in 1971, lowering the voting age from 21 years to 18 years. Still, are the civil rights of those younger than 18 years being violated because they aren't allowed to vote? No.

The original Constitution and its subsequent amendments don't prevent the national government or any state government from creating restrictions on people. What the Constitution forbids is *unreasonable* restrictions. A law prohibiting redheads from voting would be unreasonable. On the other hand, laws

prohibiting persons younger than 18 years from voting or persons younger than 16 years from driving a car appear reasonable because experience and maturity gained with age are necessary to make intelligent voters and skilled drivers.

The Choice Is Yours
Set # 3

To check your understanding of the previous material, answer the following questions by selecting the letter of the correct answer.

1. Which amendment abolished slavery?
   a. Thirteenth
   b. Twenty-Sixth
   c. Fifteenth
   d. Sixteenth

2. The following is an example of a "civil right":
   a. The right to vote
   b. The right to housing
   c. The right to job opportunities
   d. All of the above

3. What is the youngest age at which you can vote?
   a. 25
   b. 15
   c. 18
   d. 21

4. Which amendment gave women the right to vote?
   a. Nineteenth
   b. Twenty-Fifth
   c. Sixteenth
   d. None—women were always allowed to vote

5. The Due Process Clause and the Equal Protection Clause of the _____ Amendment protect citizens' liberties from possible abusive actions by state governments.
   a. Fifth
   b. Twenty-First
   c. Fourteenth
   d. Sixteenth

Projects You Can Do

Use the Internet or your public library to:

1. Find a copy of amendments eleven through twenty-seven. Which amendments address economic issues? Which deal with the procedures of government? Which guarantee civil rights?
2. Learn about the equal rights amendment, which had been proposed, but was never ratified (approved). Why didn't the country ratify it as an amendment to the Constitution?
3. Discuss how life in the United States would be different without the freedoms guaranteed by the Bill of Rights. Are there any "rights" you would add to the Bill of Rights? Why?

We've learned how and why we've created our government, as well as what the Constitution is and which rights it has given us. Now we are ready to learn about branches of government established by the Constitution. The first branch of the government we shall look at is the subject of Article I: the legislative branch.

CHAPTER FOUR

The Legislative Branch

LEGISLATIVE BRANCH

HOW THE CONGRESS WAS CREATED

As we learned in Chapter Two, the Constitution divided the new government into three branches:

- the legislative branch
- the executive branch
- the judicial branch.

The men who wrote the Constitution didn't want any person or group in the government to be too powerful. After all, they had had it with the King thing!

The Congress is the **legislative branch**, or lawmaking branch, of the federal government. Before we see how Congress is set up and what it does, let's find out why it looks like it does today.

Our current Congress is a **bicameral legislature**, which means it's divided into two houses, or parts: the House of Representatives and the Senate. Our Congress wasn't always like this. The Articles of Confederation had set up a **unicameral legislature**, meaning the Congress had only one house. State legislatures picked who was going to represent them in the Congress, and each state  was given one vote when it came to passing laws. As we learned, the Articles of Confederation didn't give this early Congress much power, and the citizens soon became unhappy because Congress wasn't able to get anything done.

When the delegates got together at the Constitutional Convention in May 1787, many of them wanted the national government to have a strong legislative group. To accomplish this, James Madison offered his Virginia Plan, which the large, more populated states supported. Part of Madison's Virginia Plan set up a bicameral legislature in which members of one house were to be elected by voters of their state, and the other house would have its members nominated (chosen) by their state's legislature.

Although the Congress set up by the Articles of Confederation had only one house, or chamber, the delegates at the

Constitutional Convention were familiar with the bicameral structure. The British Parliament consisted (and still does) of two houses: the House of Lords and the House of Commons. Also, at the time of the Constitutional Convention, the legislatures of all but two states were bicameral. The Virginia Plan wanted the number of each state's representatives in both houses to be based on its population. This meant that the more people a state had living in it, the more representatives that state earned in both houses of Congress.

Did You Know?

Rhode Island was the only state that didn't participate in the 1787 Constitutional Convention. Pennsylvania sent the most delegates.

As you might have guessed, the small, less populated states didn't like the Virginia Plan. Instead, they liked William Patterson's New Jersey Plan. The New Jersey Plan stuck with the one-house legislature. However, it strengthened the Congress by empowering it to raise money for the new country through taxes. The plan also gave Congress the power to control *interstate commerce* (the buying and selling of goods between citizens living in different states). Under the New Jersey Plan, each state had one vote, and each state legislature chose its Congressional representative.

Surf's up...

To learn more about how our Congress was created, check out these sites:

bensguide.gpo.gov/6-8/government/national/legislature.html

vote-smart.org/reference/primer/consti.phtml

However, the delegates had a problem. The states that had many people living in them wanted ***proportional representation*** (representation based on population), and the less populated states wanted ***equal representation*** (one vote per state).

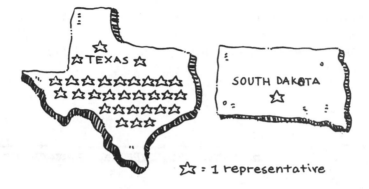

☆ = 1 representative

Roger Sherman, a delegate from Connecticut, offered a plan that made both sides happy. His plan became known as the Great Compromise, or the Connecticut Compromise. The Great Compromise suggested basing the number of each state's representatives in the House of Representatives on the population of the state. For example, today, Texas has a population of more than 21 million people, earning it the right to have 30 representatives in the House of Representatives. By comparison, South Dakota has a population of only 750,000; it has only one member in the House. Once the number was set, the voters in the state would choose their representatives. Over in the Senate, each state, no matter how many people were living in it, would have two senators, and the state's legislature would select those senators.

Most delegates voted for the compromise plan. However, no plan gave all the electing power to the citizens. The delegates at the Constitutional Convention didn't trust the people to be in complete control of picking their representatives. Under the Great Compromise, which became the new legislative structure, the citizens could only elect their representatives for the House of Representatives. The process remained like this until Congress passed the Seventeenth Amendment to the Constitution in 1913. The change occurred because of a series of scandalous elections in the late 1800s and early 1900s. Citizens felt that many of the candidates were selected because they were friends or business associates of the legislators, rather than because they were qualified. William Jennings Bryan was a congressman from Nebraska. He wanted to stamp out the special interest groups that influenced the state legislatures that selected the senators, so he convinced many other people to persuade the Congress to pass the *Seventeenth Amendment*, which allowed the citizens to elect their senators, just as they did their representatives.

Surf's up...

The Seventeenth Amendment is one of our most contested amendments. Learn more about it at this site:

bensguide.gp.gov/6-8/election/senators.html

Did You Know?

William Jennings Bryan failed in three campaigns to be elected president, but he succeeded in getting senators elected by the people, something he struggled to do for 20 years.

The Choice Is Yours
Set #1

To check your understanding of the previous material, answer the following questions by selecting the letter of the correct answer. If you want to check your work, refer to the Answer Key in the back of the book.

1. A Congress that has two parts, or houses, is referred to as a_____.
   a. unicameral legislature
   b. bicameral legislature
   c. two-party system
   d. parliament

2. The chart below shows the number of representatives for California, North Carolina, and Texas. Select the population that is closest to that of Texas if the population of California is 34,500,000 and the population of North Carolina is 8,200,000.

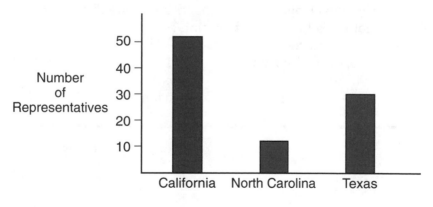

   a. 8 million
   b. 55 million
   c. 21 million
   d. 34 million

3. Roger Sherman offered a plan that came to be known as_____.
   a. the Great Compromise
   b. the Great Idea
   c. Sherman's Plan
   d. the New Jersey Plan

4. The chart below shows the number of representatives that certain states have. Which state has the largest population?

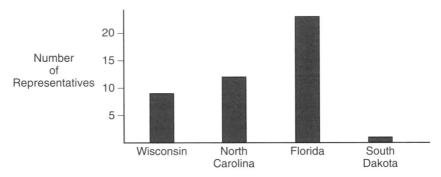

   a. Wisconsin
   b. North Carolina
   c. Florida
   d. South Dakota

5. Which constitutional amendment called for the direct election of senators by the voters of the state?
   a. First Amendment
   b. Seventeenth Amendment
   c. Tenth Amendment
   d. None—it is in the original Constitution

Things to Think About

1. What kinds of things might people living in a state with a large population disagree over with people who live in a lightly populated state?

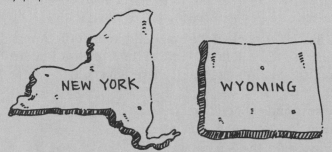

2. Can you think of a way to create a unicameral Congress that fairly represents the citizens who live in heavily populated states and the citizens who live in less populated states?
3. Why do you think the delegates to the Constitutional Convention of 1787 didn't trust the people to have complete control over electing their representatives? Do these reasons still exist today?
4. The statewide advertising campaigns necessary for candidates to run for the Senate are now very expensive. Many people believe that candidates spend too much time and money trying to get elected to the Senate, and they want to reform the system. Some suggest that if senators were elected by state legislatures, candidates wouldn't need money to campaign. So, was the Seventeenth Amendment a good idea?
5. How could Congress have prevented some of these bad consequences? Are there other ways to resolve this problem?

Projects You Can Do

Using your classmates, create your own legislature. Decide which powers your legislature will have. Is it bicameral? How are the voters represented? How does it differ from the current structure of Congress?

Now that we understand why Congress is set up like it is, let's find out what powers the Constitution gives it.

THE POWERS OF CONGRESS

If you flip to the back of the book and look at the Appendix of Documents, you will find a copy of the Constitution. Article I, Section 8, lists 27 things that Congress has the power to do:

1. Assess and collect taxes
2. Provide for the common defense
3. Provide for the general welfare
4. Borrow money on the credit of the United States
5. Regulate business with foreign countries
6. Regulate interstate commerce (the buying and selling of goods occurring between citizens living in different states)
7. Regulate commerce with Indian (Native American) tribes
8. Establish naturalization rules (rules for people born in other countries to become citizens of the United States)
9. Establish bankruptcy laws (laws to help people or businesses who can no longer pay their debts)
10. Coin and regulate the value of money
11. Regulate the value of foreign money in the United States
12. Fix the standard of weights and measures
13. Punish counterfeiters (people who make fake money)
14. Establish post offices

15. Promote the progress of science and useful arts
16. Establish patents (legal right that protects inventors from other people stealing their idea) and copyrights (legal right protecting musicians and writers from people stealing their songs or stories)
17. Establish the federal courts system
18. Punish piracy on the high seas

19. Punish offenses against the laws of nations
20. Declare war
21. Raise and support an army
22. Provide and maintain a navy
23. Regulate the land and naval forces
24. Call the militia (National Guard) to suppress insurrections (rebellions) and repel (stop) invasions
25. Organize and arm the militia
26. Govern the District of Columbia
27. Build forts, docks, and other buildings on government property

   We call these powers listed in Article I, Section 8, the *enumerated powers*. Other parts of the Constitution and later amendments assign Congress additional powers, such as the power to:

- admit new states to the United States (Article IV, Section 3)
- propose amendments to the Constitution (Article V)
- collect federal income taxes (Sixteenth Amendment)
- ensure civil rights (Thirteenth, Fifteenth, Nineteenth, Twenty-Fourth, and Twenty-Sixth Amendments). Civil rights protect people from national and state governments discriminating against them because of their race, religion, sex, age, or ethnic origin.
- determine whether a president is mentally or emotionally disabled and thus unable to continue in office (Twenty-Fifth Amendment).

Surf's up...

Learn more about Congress's enumerated powers at these sites:

vote-smart.org/reference/primer/clead.phtml
4dnet.com/~wongway/congress/powers.html

The Choice Is Yours
Set # 2

To check your understanding of the previous material, answer the following questions by selecting the letter of the correct answer.

1. Where in the Constitution are most of the powers of Congress enumerated?
   a. Article II
   b. Article III, Section 1
   c. Article I, Section 8
   d. Article I, Section 1

2. How many powers are enumerated in the above section?
   a. 10
   b. 20
   c. 27
   d. 35

3. Which of the following is not an enumerated (written in the Constitution) power of Congress?
   a. Provide for the common defense
   b. Declare war
   c. Establish post offices
   d. Command the Army and Navy

4. Article V gives Congress another enumerated power—that is, the power to_____.
   a. collect federal income taxes
   b. enforce Civil Rights Laws
   c. propose amendments to the Constitution
   d. govern the District of Columbia

5. Congress is given the power to punish counterfeiters. Counterfeiters are people who_____.
   a. sing badly
   b. print fake money
   c. don't vote
   d. steal stories from writers

MORE THAN WHAT'S ON THE PAPER

The Constitution doesn't mention all the powers that Congress exercises today. Even so, Congress has the right to exercise these powers because they are necessary for it to do its job. We call these necessary (but unmentioned) powers *implied powers*. If you look at the end of Article I, Section 8, you will see that the Constitution gives Congress the right to make all laws "necessary and proper" to carry out its enumerated powers. We refer to this sentence as the *Elastic Clause* because it stretches the authority of Congress, providing Congress with whatever additional powers it needs to do its work. That means Congress

can create these unmentioned powers that it feels are necessary to carry out its enumerated powers. Thomas Jefferson was opposed to the clause because he was concerned it would give Congress too much power. Nevertheless, Alexander Hamilton convinced the framers to insert the clause. However, the debate still goes on today. The following are just a few examples of the powers that Congress has given itself through the Elastic Clause.

Surf's up...

Glide into these sites and see
what some are saying about
Congress's implied powers and the Elastic Clause:

ghaskell.com/socsci/civimpliedpowers.htm

conlaw.usatoday.findlaw.com/constitution/
article01/44.htm

Some Elastic Clause powers

- Congress established a national banking system under the power to tax and borrow.
- Congress regulates the railroads and the airlines under the power to set up post offices and roads.
- Congress has passed laws regulating how businesses conducting interstate commerce pay and treat their employees based on their enumerated power to regulate interstate commerce.

Projects You Can Do

1. Congress created the Federal Aviation Agency (FAA) and the Federal Deposit Insurance Corporation (FDIC), using its power under the Elastic Clause. Use the Internet or your public library to learn about these government agencies. What functions do they perform? Are the functions of these agencies necessary? Are there other ways of performing these functions?
2. Almost every taxpayer complains about paying federal income tax each year. Use the Internet or you local library to learn more about the Sixteenth Amendment, as well as the history of and the reasons for collecting federal income tax.

3. Select and research one of the following enumerated powers:
   - fix the standard of weights and measures
   - coin and regulate the value of money
   - establish post offices.

A Minute with Senator WordSmart
Set # 1

We've seen how Congress was created and what powers it was given. Take a minute to make sure that you understand the meanings of the new words. Match the word in the left-hand column with its definition in the right-hand column by drawing a line from the word to its definition. If you want to check your work, review the Answer Key in the back of the book.

1. Legislative branch

2. Bicameral legislature

3. Proportional representation
4. Equal representation

5. Seventeenth Amendment

6. Interstate commerce

7. Enumerated powers

a. The powers intended to be given by the Constitution to Congress, but not stated.

b. The last sentence of Article I, Section 8. It stretches the power of Congress.

c. Equal votes per state.
d. The buying and selling of goods across state lines.

e. Voting power based on population.

f. Requires direct election of senators by the voters of the state.

g. Specifically mentioned powers in the Constitution.

8. Implied powers

9. Elastic Clause

h. The lawmaking branch of government.

i. A legislature with two houses, or parts.

Did You Know?

Unlike the United States, the British don't have a document called a Constitution. However, we say that the British have a constitutional government because their lawmakers are subject to defined, written restraints. They just don't appear in a single document.

Although our modern Congress has much more power than the original Congress, its power is still limited, compared with the ruling bodies in other countries. This is the way the writers of the Constitution wanted it. For example, Article I, Section 9, says that our Congress cannot:

- arrest people and keep them in jail without a reason. (Those imprisoned are entitled to "the privilege of the writ of habeas corpus." This is the right of the imprisoned to ask a judge to command the police to explain the reason for the imprisonment.)

- pass special acts that punish someone for a crime without a jury trial (called a "bill of attainder").
- pass a law that punishes a person for doing something that was legal when the person did it (called an "ex post facto" law).
- put a tax on a person (called a "head tax").
- tax products produced in one state and sold in another.
- favor the shipping ports and harbors of one state over another.
- tax ships sailing from one state to another.
- spend money without first having a budget for the country.
- grant titles of nobility (such as "king" or "queen").

Things to Think About

1. The Elastic Clause, which is a portion of Article I, Section 8, reads, in part, "to make all laws which shall be necessary and proper for carrying into execution the foregoing powers and all other powers vested by the constitution in the government of the United States or in any Department or Officer thereof." Looking at the specific examples of Congress interpreting the Elastic Clause, do you think the clause is too elastic? That is, has the Congress taken too much power?
2. Why did the writers of the Constitution add the Elastic Clause to the Constitution?
3. Why is only Congress allowed to declare war?
4. Why do you think the writers of the Constitution didn't want Congress to have the powers mentioned in Article I, Section 9?

We've seen what Congress has been given the power to do, and what it isn't allowed to do. Now, let's look at the powers that the Constitution has given to only one house of the legislature. We call these *exclusive powers*.

EXCLUSIVE POWERS OF THE SENATE AND THE HOUSE

As mentioned earlier, only the House of Representatives may introduce bills to raise government revenue (that is, collect taxes). Also, only the House has the power to:

- *impeach* (bring charges against) federal officials for misconduct. However, once the House has impeached the official, the Senate alone has the power to convict and remove the official from office.
- elect the president, if no presidential candidate earns a majority in the electoral college. The electoral college is the body of electors from the states chosen to elect the president and the vice president. The Senate is in charge of electing the vice president.

On the other hand, only the Senate can approve:

- presidential nominations or selections for ambassadorships (our official representatives to other countries),
- judges serving in the federal courts, and
- members of the cabinet (official advisors to the president of the United States).

Also, only the Senate can approve treaties (official agreements between the United States and foreign countries). Finally, only the Senate can try a government official accused of committing a crime against the United States.

Now that we understand the powers of Congress, let's see how Congress is set up to use those powers.

The Choice Is Yours
Set # 3

To check your understanding of the previous material, answer the following questions by selecting the letter of the correct answer.

1. Only the _____ has the power to impeach federal officials.
   a. House of Representatives
   b. Senate
   c. president
   d. Supreme Court

2. Only the _____ can approve treaties.
   a. president
   b. Supreme Court
   c. House of Representatives
   d. Senate

3. Only the _____ can introduce legislation into Congress that raises revenue.
   a. president
   b. Supreme Court
   c. House of Representatives
   d. Senate

4. Only the _____ can approve federal court judges.
   a. president
   b. Supreme Court
   c. House of Representatives
   d. Senate

5. Only the _____ can remove an impeached federal official.
   a. president
   b. Supreme Court
   c. House of Representatives
   d. Senate

THE STRUCTURE OF CONGRESS

The Great Compromise of 1787 caused the two chambers of Congress to differ in a number of ways. The most obvious way they differ is in the number of members. The Senate has 100 members (two senators from each state). By contrast, the House of Representatives has 435 members, a number fixed by the Reapportionment Act of 1929.

Each elected member in the House represents individual *congressional districts*. Each state has been divided into congressional districts, which are areas that contain nearly the same number of people. That means the congressional districts in big cities are smaller in area than the congressional districts in less densely populated rural (country) areas. Although the population of our country has increased over the years, the Reapportionment Act recognized that simply adding more representatives to the House would make it too crowded to be effective.

The government takes the *national census* every ten years (the last one was in 2000). They count the number of people living in the United States, as well as where they live within their states. After each national census, the boundaries of the congressional districts are adjusted, but not the total number of representatives.

Redrawing the boundaries of congressional districts so that each district has roughly the same number of people within its boundaries is known as *reapportionment*. Reapportionment is the responsibility of the state legislatures. Today, each member of the House represents about 655,000 people. The following table shows how many representatives each state is entitled to. Find out how may representatives your state has.

State	Number of Representatives
Alabama	7
Alaska	1
Arizona	6
Arkansas	4
California	52
Colorado	6
Connecticut	6
Delaware	1
Florida	23
Georgia	11
Hawaii	2
Idaho	2
Illinois	20
Indiana	10
Iowa	5
Kansas	4
Kentucky	6
Louisiana	7
Maine	2
Maryland	8
Massachusetts	10
Michigan	16
Minnesota	8
Mississippi	5
Missouri	9

State	Number of Representatives
Montana	1
Nebraska	3
Nevada	2
New Hampshire	2
New Jersey	13
New Mexico	3
New York	31
North Carolina	12
North Dakota	1
Ohio	19
Oklahoma	6
Oregon	5
Pennsylvania	21
Rhode Island	2
South Carolina	6
South Dakota	1
Tennessee	9
Texas	30
Utah	3
Vermont	1
Virginia	11
Washington	9
West Virginia	3
Wisconsin	9
Wyoming	1

Projects You Can Do

Use the Internet or your local library to:

1. Research the history of the growth or decline of your state's representation.
2. Learn the boundaries of your congressional district. How were the boundaries determined, and who determined them?
3. Learn how a census is taken. How can citizens participate in this once-in-a-decade event?

Equal, but different

This discussion brings up a difference between the Senate and the House of Representatives. A senator's *constituency*—the people represented—is likely to be more diverse (different) than a House member's is. A congressional district usually covers only a small part of the state (unless the representative lives in a sparsely populated state, such as North Dakota or Wyoming).

Did You Know?

Five additional representatives—one each, from Puerto Rico, Guam, American Samoa, the Virgin Islands, and the District of Columbia—represent their constituencies in the House. Although they may participate in much of the work, they aren't allowed to vote.

A Minute with Senator WordSmart
Set # 2

We've learned more about how Congress is structured. Take a minute and review the meanings of some new words. Match the word with its definition.

1. Impeach

2. Congressional district

3. National census

4. Reapportionment

5. Constituency

a. The people represented by an elected official.

b. To bring charges against a federal official for wrongdoing.

c. The effort to count the number of people in the United States and determine where they live.

d. The geographical area and its people represented by a member of the House of Representatives.

e. The redrawing of boundaries of a congressional district.

For either house of Congress to be able to do its job, it must have effective leadership. Let's see how the legislative branch organizes its leadership.

CONGRESSIONAL LEADERSHIP

The House of Representatives

An elected leader of the ***majority political party*** (the political party with the most members in that house of Congress) controls each house of Congress. For example, the House of Representatives is presided over or supervised by the ***Speaker of the House***, which is an important job. The Speaker, who is elected by the other party representatives, runs the day-to-day business of the House and selects members to fill various leadership positions. Also, the Speaker is next in line after the vice president to take over the presidency. That means if the president and vice president die or are otherwise unable to serve, the Speaker will automatically be appointed president.

The ***majority floor leader***, who ranks behind the Speaker, also belongs to the majority political party. The majority floor leader is elected through a ***caucus***, a meeting of the House party members. The leader presents the party's official position on issues and tries to persuade the party members to vote the same way.

The ***minority political party*** (the party that doesn't have the majority of members in the House) also has a leader. We call this party's leader the ***minority floor leader***, and that person is the party's spokesperson. Like the majority floor leader, the minority floor leader tries to persuade party members to vote the same way on issues. If the minority party wins a majority of the seats in the next congressional election, the minority floor leader usually becomes the majority floor leader.

Surf's up...

If you want to learn more about the leadership positions in the House of Representatives, this site is for you:

bensguide.gpo.gov/6-8/government/national.html

The Senate

The Constitution appoints the vice president of the United States *president of the Senate*. In recent years, however, vice presidents have usually presided only on ceremonial occasions or at meetings of special importance. In fact, Article I, Section 3, of the Constitution permits the vice president to vote only when the senators are deadlocked (tied) on a vote. To deal with the daily business, the Senate chooses the *president pro tempore*, which means "temporary president." This position usually goes to the senator in the majority political party who has served the longest. The president pro tempore presides over the Senate or, more typically, gives the new senators of both parties turns at presiding over the Senate. The Senate also chooses a *majority leader* to schedule the majority political party's proposed legislation and a *minority leader*, who helps the minority political party with this responsibility.

Surf's up...

**Leading the Senate is a topic
of these sites:**

senate.gov/learning/learn_how_2.html

**bensguide.gop.gov/
6-8/government/national/senate.html**

In both the House and the Senate, the majority and minority party leaders select *whips*, or members who round up the other members to vote on important legislation. The whips also help provide information so that their fellow members know their party's position on upcoming proposed legislation.

A Minute with Senator WordSmart
Set # 3

We've just read about the leadership positions in Congress. Take a minute to review the meanings of some new words related to this leadership.

1. Majority political party
2. Speaker of the House
3. Majority floor leader

a. The political party with the most members in a house of Congress.
b. A meeting of House of Representatives party members.
c. The leaders in Congress who round up fellow legislators to vote on important bills.

4. Caucus

5. Minority political party

6. Minority floor leader

7. President pro tempore

8. Senate majority leader

9. Senate minority leader

10. Whips

d. The leader chosen by senators of the majority political party to schedule proposed legislation.

e. The political party that doesn't have the most members in a house of Congress.

f. The leader chosen by senators of the minority political party to schedule proposed legislation.

g. The temporary President of the Senate.

h. Presents the official position of the majority political party regarding proposed legislation. Second in rank to the Speaker of the House.

i. Presents the official position of the minority party regarding proposed legislation.

j. Supervises the House of Representatives.

The congressional leadership and the rest of the Congress must answer to the voters. If the voters are unhappy with their congressional representatives, they can show it by voting them out of office.

ELECTIONS

For the House of Representatives

The Constitution sets out the qualifications a person must have to run for election to the House of Representatives. Article I, Section 2, states that a person must be at least 25 years old and have been a citizen of the United States for at least seven years. The candidate must live in the state when elected, and custom now requires that the candidate also live in the congressional district that that person wishes to represent.

The entire House of Representatives must run for reelection every two years. The writers of the Constitution designed the House to be the most responsive to the wants of the voters. Frequent elections were designed to ensure that House members consider what their constituents want when voting on proposed legislation. For that reason, the writers gave the House the sole power to introduce legislation that would raise taxes. Remember: "No taxation without representation" was the seed that grew into the American Revolution.

For the Senate

Because senators serve six-year staggered terms, meaning the terms do not all begin at the same time, only one-third of the senators must run for reelection every two years. This means that the Senate is a less-changing body than the House because two-thirds of the Senate's membership remain unchanged, regardless of who is elected.

A candidate for the Senate, according to Article I, Section 3, must be at least 30 years old and have been a citizen for at least nine years. The candidate must live within the state that person wants to represent.

	House of Representatives	Senate
Minimum Age	25 years old	30 years old
U.S. Citizenship	at least 7 years	at least 9 years
Residence	within the state; but usually, within the congressional district	within the state
Elected Term	2 years	6 years

Elections for both houses are held on the first Tuesday after the first Monday in November of even-numbered years, or on special dates set by state laws to fill seats that become vacant between terms.

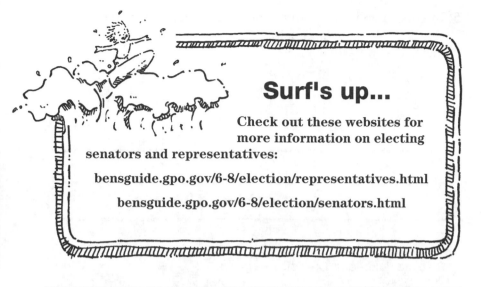

Surf's up...

Check out these websites for more information on electing senators and representatives:

bensguide.gpo.gov/6-8/election/representatives.html

bensguide.gpo.gov/6-8/election/senators.html

The Choice Is Yours
Set # 4

To check your understanding of the previous material, answer the following questions by selecting the letter of the correct answer.

1. The minimum age for a senator is _____ years old.
   a. 25
   b. 30
   c. 35
   d. 40

2. The minimum age for a representative in the House of Representatives is _____ years old.
   a. 25
   b. 30
   c. 35
   d. 40

3. The term of a senator is _____ years.
   a. 2
   b. 3
   c. 4
   d. 6

4. The term of a representative is _____ years.
   a. 2
   b. 3
   c. 4
   d. 6

5. A candidate for the Senate must have lived in the United States for _____ years before running for office.
   a. 6
   b. 9
   c. 15
   d. 2

Things to Think About

1. Why does the Constitution require that candidates for the Senate live in their home state? Why is it traditional for candidates for the House to live in the districts they wish to represent?
2. What are some reasons for and against limiting the number of elected terms that a senator or a representative may serve?
3. Are there other minimum qualifications that you would add? For example, would you include level of education?
4. What are the advantages of a six-year term compared with a two-year term? What are the disadvantages?
5. Below is a chart of the number of women in Congress in 1947, 1987, and 2002. Compare the increase from 1947 to 1987 (40 years) with the increase from 1987 to 2002 (just 15 years). What do the charts tell you? Why is the percentage increasing? Do you think this percentage will continue to increase? Why or why not?

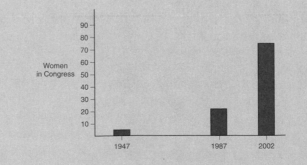

Projects You Can Do

Use the Internet or your local library to:

1. Find out:

   - Who is the Speaker of the House?
   - Who is your representative, and what is your congressional district?
   - Who are your senators? Write a short biography on each one.

2. Pick a country that has a legislature. What are the minimum qualifications for being a legislator in that country?
3. List the personal qualities, educational background, and other characteristics you feel are necessary for a person to hold the office of Senator. Provide reasons for selecting these personal characteristics. Compare your list and reasons to those of your classmates.

WHEN DO THEY MEET?

Congress meets in **sessions**. The Twentieth Amendment, adopted in 1933, requires that both houses meet at noon on the third day of January after the November elections to organize the upcoming **biennium** (two-year period). One session is held each year, extending continuously from January until adjournment (ending) in fall. Each biennium is called a "Congress." The First Congress was held from 1789–1790.

Did You Know?

Most of the time the House and the Senate each meet in their own chamber in the U.S. Capitol in Washington, D.C. However, every once in a while, they must meet together (joint session). For example, a joint session is needed to count the electoral votes in presidential elections. Joint sessions are held in the House chamber.

Things to Think About

1. Why do you think the Congress is not in session all year long?
2. Why do you think the congressional sessions are 2 years long?

As the legislative branch, Congress's main purpose is to make laws. This next section shows us how it goes about doing that.

MAKING OF THE LAWS

Usually, people make their best decisions when they take the time to gather all available information and think about a problem. That's why the writers of the Constitution wanted Congress to take their time when they made laws; they wanted Congress to gather all available information and think about the problem before passing a law about it. Therefore, the legislative process created in the Constitution is slow and complicated. The process is also designed to encourage **compromise**, by each side agreeing to some things the other side wants. We will see that a proposed law, or **bill**, must travel through a series of steps before it becomes a law, providing time for gathering information, thinking, and compromising.

Thousands of bills are introduced in Congress each year. However, most don't survive the following process, so they don't become laws. Let's look at the process, step-by-step.

Step 1. Introduce the proposed legislation

Except for revenue or tax bills, which can come only from the House of Representatives, any member of the House or Senate can introduce a bill or proposed legislation. We call the member who introduces the bill the *sponsor of the bill*. A bill may have numerous cosponsors. Sometimes, a representative and a senator will sponsor identical bills in their own houses.

Who thinks up and writes these bills? The executive branch (the president's advisors and staff) writes many of the bills. Members of Congress, usually through their staffs, also write legislation. Commonly, an *interest group* (an organized group of people who feel strongly about an issue) that wants a particular law passed will work with the congressional staff to introduce a bill.

In the House of Representatives, the sponsor of the bill introduces the legislation by dropping the bill into the *hopper*, which is the box on the House clerk's desk meant to hold newly proposed legislation. The *House clerk* is responsible for keeping track of all proposed legislation.

In the Senate, the *presiding officer* (the senator in charge of the Senate when the bill is introduced) must recognize a sponsor of a bill so that person can introduce the bill.

Once the bill is recognized, it is assigned a number and the prefix "HR" (if it came from the House) or "S" (if it came from the Senate). The sponsor's name is also written on the bill. The bill is then sent to the Government Printing Office, where copies are made for the other members.

> ## Things to Think About
>
> 1. Why is it a good idea to have a set procedure for introducing legislation?
> 2. Do you think it's a good idea that each senator and representative has the right to introduce bills?
> 3. If you were a member of an interest group, how would you try to persuade your legislator to vote in your favor?

Step 2. Send the bill to the appropriate committee

As mentioned earlier, Congress considers thousands of bills during each session. Because it is impossible for each Congressperson to become an expert on the issues concerning each introduced bill, *standing committees* study the sponsored legislation. Standing committees are small groups of legislators who have specialized areas of knowledge. These permanent committees decide whether the bill should be presented to the full chamber.

The committee system allows Congress to research an area of public policy and hear from interested parties, and it allows committee members to become knowledgeable on important topics so they can share this knowledge with the rest of Congress. The committees serve as minilegislatures, performing the task of investigating and debating bills that, because of lack of time, would never be considered by the full chamber. As mentioned, party leaders decide which members will serve on a particular committee. Their decision is based, in part, on the expertise and seniority of the member. Most House members only serve on one committee; all senators serve on several.

The following table lists the standing committees in the Senate and in the House of Representatives. The House has 20 standing committees, and the Senate has 16. Notice that both chambers have standing committees in some of the same areas. That's because these are important areas, so they see a lot of proposed legislation.

House of Representatives Standing Committees	Senate Standing Committees
1. Agriculture	1. Agriculture, Nutrition, and Forestry
2. Appropriations	2. Appropriations
3. Armed Services	3. Armed Services
4. Budget	4. Banking, Housing, and Urban Affairs
5. Education and the Workforce	5. Budget
6. Energy and Commerce	6. Commerce, Science, and Transportation
7. Financial Services	7. Energy and Natural Resources
8. Government Reform	8. Environment and Public Works
9. House Administration	9. Finance
10. International Relations	10. Foreign Relations
11. Judiciary	11. Governmental Affairs
12. Resources	12. Judiciary
13. Rules	13. Health, Education, Labor, and Pensions
14. Science	14. Rules and Administration
15. Small Business	15. Small Business
16. Standards of Official Conduct	16. Veterans' Affairs
17. Transportation and Infrastructure	
18. Veterans' Affairs	
19. Ways and Means	
20. Intelligence	

Surf's up...

Committees are where it's at!
Learn more about them at
these sites:

house.gov/house/CommitteeWWW.html
senate.gov/committees/index.cfm

In the House, the Speaker assigns the new bill to the proper standing committee. In the Senate, the presiding officer schedules the bills. Some bills are complex and have to be sent to more than one standing committee, in which case, the bill is divided so that its parts can be sent to different committees. To schedule their review, bills are placed on the calendar of the committee to which they have been assigned. If the committee decides not to consider the bill, the bill stops in the process and has no chance of becoming a law.

Did You Know?

Do you think that Congress has a lot of committees now? In 1913, the two houses had 135 committees! Enough was enough. Congress decided to streamline the committee system and passed the Legislative Reorganization Act of 1946.

The Choice Is Yours
Set # 5

To check your understanding of the previous material, answer the following questions by selecting the letter of the correct answer.

1. The legislator who introduces a bill is referred to as the bill's _____.
   a. creator
   b. writer
   c. sponsor
   d. owner

2. A bill known as "HR-Jones" designates _____.
   a. a home run by Jones
   b. a bill originating in the House of Representatives and sponsored by Jones
   c. that Jones is the presiding officer of the Senate
   d. a bill originating in the Senate and sponsored by Jones

HR-JONES

3. Which of the following isn't a standing committee in the House of Representatives?
   a. Science
   b. Intelligence
   c. Foreign Relations
   d. Government Reform

4. The legislative process is designed to be _____.
   a. slow and deliberate
   b. efficient
   c. quick and easy
   d. so complicated that no one can understand it

5. The legislative process is also designed to create _____.
   a. boredom
   b. a lot of noise
   c. compromise
   d. confusion

If the committee decides to consider the bill, it assigns the bill to a ***subcommittee***, a smaller group within the standing committee. The subcommittee studies the bill by holding hearings (meetings arranged by the Congress with different groups so that Congress can learn about a particular topic) on the bill. At these hearings, the subcommittee members listen to supporters and opponents of the proposed legislation. After the hearings, the subcommittee members will ***markup*** the bill—that is, change, amend, and possibly rewrite sections or the entire bill, creating what is referred to as a ***committee print***. The subcommittee then votes on the final version of the bill. If it approves the bill, it sends the revised bill back to committee, where the whole process of hearings, markup, and voting are repeated.

A Minute with Senator WordSmart
Set # 4

We've learned many new terms regarding introducing a bill in Congress.

1. Sponsor of the bill

2. Interest group

3. Bill
4. Hopper

a. A smaller group within the standing committee who studies the bill.

b. A small group of legislators who have specialized areas of knowledge. The group has been permanently established to determine whether proposed legislation in their specialized area should be presented to the entire House or the entire Senate for review.

c. A legislator who introduces a bill.

d. The box on the House clerk's desk that holds newly proposed legislation.

5. Standing committee   e. To rewrite, amend, and edit a bill.
6. Subcommittee   f. An organized group of people who feel strongly about an issue and who want legislation passed concerning that issue.
7. Markup   g. Proposed legislation.
8. Session   h. A two-year period.
9. Biennium   i. The time, each year, from January through fall when Congress meets.

Step 3. Prepare the bill for debate in the sponsor's chamber

Whenever the Senate committee approves a bill, it is ready to be put on the calendar for debate. The bill's sponsors schedule when the debate will begin through a *unanimous consent agreement*.

In the House, bills are placed on one of four calendars:

- The *Union Calendar* schedules bills that will raise revenues (taxes) and spending bills (appropriations).
- The *House Calendar* schedules bills that won't raise revenue or need money or property.
- The *Consent Calendar* schedules bills that aren't controversial and will be passed without debate.
- The *Private Calendar* schedules bills that require the United States to pay money to a person or a group of people.

Things to Think About

1. Why does Congress use standing committees to consider legislation? Can you think of a better way to consider bills?
2. Can you name some interest groups? What do they do?
3. Check through the newspaper. Find an article about a bill Congress is considering. What is the bill about? Who seems to be for it? Why? Who seems to be opposed to it? Why?

Step 4. Debate the bill in the sponsoring member's chamber

The bill is now ready to be debated in the sponsoring member's chamber. Those for and against the bill will have a chance to explain their reasons and persuade others. Procedures for a floor debate in the two chambers are quite different. Because the membership of the House of Representatives is so large, the time for debate and amending the bills must be limited. Here, bills must first go through the ***Rules Committee***, a standing committee that decides:

- when the full House will debate on the bill
- if the bill can be amended during the debate process
- how much time will be allowed for each representative to speak during the debate (often five minutes or less).

Because the Rules Committee controls the important parts of the law-making process, it is probably the most powerful committee in the House. For example, the Rules Committee can defeat a bill just by:

- delaying a vote, making the representatives lose interest.
- making it easy for opponents of the bill to add ***killer amendments***, which are additions to the bill that they know will make other representatives not want to vote for the bill.

The Rules Committee can also help pass a bill by making it easy to add ***sweetener amendments***. Sweetener amendments are the opposite of killer amendments. These are additions to the bill that members who are undecided or against the bill will like, so they will, hopefully, change their minds and vote for the bill.

Did You Know?

Only 15 representatives make up the Rules Committee; 10 are from the majority party, and 5 are from the minority party.

In the Senate, which has many fewer members, fewer rules are needed. For example, there is no time limit on debate. In the extreme, a senator who wants to delay action on a bill or defeat it altogether may use a method called a *filibuster*. The senator hogs the floor by speaking for hours.

During this time, the senator will only let other senators speak who agree. A filibuster can be stopped only through *cloture*, a request for limited debate. However, at least 16 senators must agree to bring up a cloture vote. If that occurs, 60 senators must actually vote to approve the cloture, ending the filibuster. Even then, each senator can still speak for one hour.

Did You Know?

Strom Thurmond, a senator from South Carolina, holds the unofficial record for the longest filibuster. In 1957, he spoke for more than 24 hours straight on the Senate floor to block consideration of a civil rights bill!

The Senate doesn't limit the subject of the proposed amendments to a bill, like the House does. Amendments completely unrelated to the bill are called **riders**, and these riders can effectively defeat a bill. For example, a bill proposing to raise taxes to build new highways may have an amendment attached to it, reducing the quality standards for beef. Therefore, a senator who is in favor of building new highways but against reducing the beef quality standards will vote against the bill.

A Minute with Senator WordSmart
Set # 5

Before we vote on the bill in the sponsoring chamber, let's review some new terms related to debating bills. Refer to the Answer Key in the back of the book, if you want to check your work.

1. Rules Committee

2. Union Calendar

3. Cloture

4. Sweetener amendment

5. Filibuster

6. Riders

a. Amendments completely unrelated to the bill under consideration.

b. A tactic that allows a senator to speak for a long time to kill interest in a bill.

c. The procedure used to stop a filibuster.

d. A standing committee in the House of Representatives responsible for the legislative process.

e. An amendment to a bill designed to grant a benefit to potential bill supporters.

f. The calendar for taxing and spending bills.

Step 5. Vote in the sponsor's chamber

Bills are voted on in the House or Senate in several ways:

- by *voice vote* (either "aye" or "no").
- by *standing vote* (members must stand up to indicate "yes" or "no").
- by *roll call vote* (each member's vote for or against is recorded).

A bill will pass the Senate if a majority (51 out of 100 senators) votes for it. In the House, a bill will pass if a majority (218 out of 435 representatives) votes for it.

If the bill is defeated in the sponsoring chamber, it goes no further. If the bill is passed and a similar bill hasn't passed in the other chamber, the bill is sent to the other chamber, where the entire process begins all over again.

What if the other chamber has passed a similar bill? If the House and Senate pass similar bills, these bills are sent to *conference committee*. The conference committee tries to sort out the differences between the bills and writes a *compromise bill*—a bill a majority of senators and representatives will vote for. Members of both the House and Senate who have worked on the bill in their respective standing committees serve on the conference committee. Once the conference committee agrees on a compromise bill, the bill is ready to be voted on in both the House and Senate.

The Choice Is Yours
Set # 6

To check your understanding of the previous material, answer the following questions by selecting the letter of the correct answer.

1. Which of the following amendments to a bill dealing with funding the space station is a rider?
   a. An amendment to provide for additional training for astronauts
   b. An amendment to build additional roads at the Space Center
   c. An amendment that adds a federal tax to apples
   d. An amendment that provides financial aid to college engineering departments

2. The chart below shows the votes for bills a through d in the House of Representatives. Which bill(s) passed?

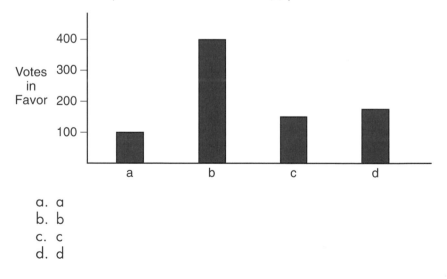

   a. a
   b. b
   c. c
   d. d

3. The chart below shows the votes for bills a through d in the Senate. Which bill(s) passed?

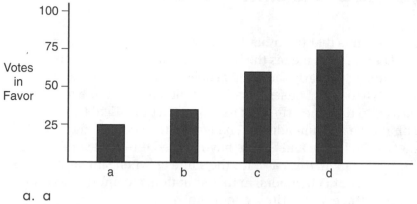

   a. a
   b. b
   c. c
   d. d

4. The _____ is charged with working out a compromise bill.
   a. Senate
   b. House of Representatives
   c. conference committee
   d. president

5. The chart below shows how long each senator spoke on the Senate floor. Which senator was filibustering?

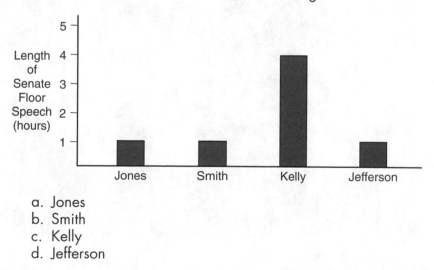

   a. Jones
   b. Smith
   c. Kelly
   d. Jefferson

Step 6. Review the bill after it has been passed by the other chamber

Let's assume that the other legislative chamber hasn't passed a similar bill. That means the bill passed in the one chamber must now undergo nearly the same process in the other chamber. Even when both houses pass a bill that started in one house and moved to the other, the bills usually aren't identical because of committee and amendment changes in the second chamber. This means the House and Senate have passed different versions of the same bill. In this case, it's the same as when similar bills are passed in both chambers. In that situation, a conference committee must meet and write a compromise bill.

Did You Know?

Legislators often vote for each other's bills when the bill doesn't affect their constituency. This is known as logrolling.

Step 7. Both chambers vote on the compromise bill

As before, once the compromise bill is approved, it is ready to be voted on by the House and the Senate. If the bill is defeated in one chamber, it dies there. However, if it passes in one chamber, it still must pass in the other chamber.

Things to Think About

1. What is the purpose of a filibuster? Do you think giving senators this right is a good idea?
2. Riders are amendments completely unrelated to the bills under consideration. Do they hurt or help the legislative process? Can you give examples?
3. Why does the House of Representatives have a Rules Committee? Why is this committee so important?
4. Why doesn't the Senate have a Rules Committee? Should it?

Step 8. Send the Congress-approved bill to the president

If both chambers pass the bill, the Speaker of the House and the president of the Senate sign it and send it to the president of the United States, who may sign (approve) or *veto* (turn down) the proposed legislation. The bill becomes a law if the president signs it. If the president doesn't act on a bill (either sign it or veto it) within ten days of receiving it (assuming Congress is still in session), the bill automatically becomes a law. On the other hand, if Congress adjourns (ends the session) before the ten days and the president hasn't signed the bill, then it doesn't become a law (called a *pocket veto*).

Did You Know?

Only about 5 percent of the bills introduced in Congress become laws.

A bill can't become a law if the president vetoes it, unless Congress **overrides the veto**. If the president vetoes the bill, it is sent back to Congress with a note listing the reasons. The chamber that originated the legislation can attempt to override the veto. First, two-thirds of those present must vote to override. Once that is accomplished, then the other chamber votes on whether to override the veto. A presidential veto is overridden when two-thirds of those voting in both the House and the Senate vote to do so. Once Congress overrides the presidential veto, the bill becomes a law.

Surf's up...

Want to learn more about how Congress passes laws? Check out these sites:

congress.indiana.edu/learn_about/legislate.htm

bensguide.gpo.gov/6-8/lawmaking/index.html

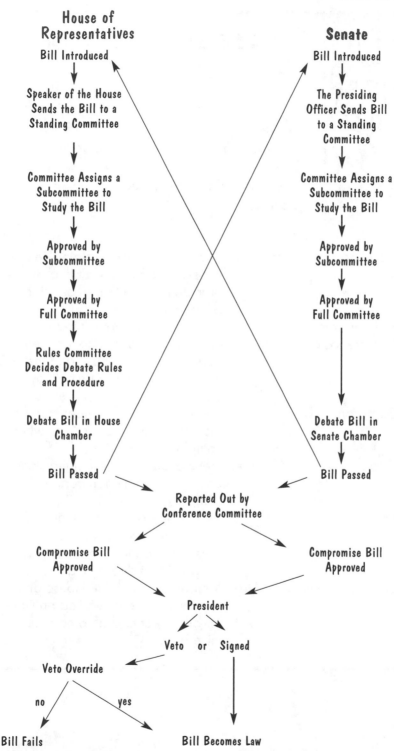

House of
Representatives

Senate

Bill Introduced

Speaker of the House
Sends the Bill to a
Standing Committee

Committee Assigns a
Subcommittee to
Study the Bill

Approved by
Subcommittee

Approved by
Full Committee

Rules Committee
Decides Debate Rules
and Procedure

Debate Bill in House
Chamber

Bill Passed

Bill Introduced

The Presiding
Officer Sends Bill
to a Standing
Committee

Committee Assigns a
Subcommittee to
Study the Bill

Approved by
Subcommittee

Approved by
Full Committee

Debate Bill in
Senate Chamber

Bill Passed

Reported Out by
Conference Committee

Compromise Bill
Approved

Compromise Bill
Approved

President

Veto   or   Signed

Veto Override

no   yes

Bill Fails

Bill Becomes Law

A Minute with Senator WordSmart
Set # 6

We've seen the voting process and how the president can defeat legislation that Congress has passed. Let's review some new terms related to this part of the process.

1. Standing vote

    a. Two-thirds of the legislators in both houses vote to pass a bill over the president's rejection, making the bill a law.

2. Roll call vote

    b. Each member's vote is recorded.

3. Conference committee

    c. A bill that satisfies enough members in both the House and the Senate to have it approved by both chambers.

4. Compromise bill

    d. Members of the chamber stand to indicate their "yes" or "no" when voting on a bill.

5. Veto

    e. Presidential rejection of legislation passed by both chambers of Congress.

6. Pocket veto

    f. If Congress adjourns before 10 days have passed since a bill was presented to the president, and the president doesn't sign the bill.

7. Override the veto

    g. Members of both the House and Senate who have worked on similar bills meet to draft a compromise bill.

Things to Think About

1. Why do most bills fail to become laws?
2. If you were on a conference committee, what things would you consider when writing a compromise bill? Why?

Projects You Can Do

1. Invite a Congressperson to speak to your class. Ask the representative to describe a particular piece of legislation, whether it passed, and what its effects are likely to be.
2. Invite a guest speaker from a special interest group to your class to talk about the group's objectives. Ask the speaker to explain how the group presents their issues to Congress.
3. Create your own Congress; half the class can be the Senate, and the other half can be the House of Representatives. Introduce, debate, and pass a bill. Create a committee to write a compromise bill.

Although Congress's main task is to make laws, it has other equally important tasks. This next section discusses some of these important *nonlegislative* (nonlawmaking) tasks.

NONLEGISLATIVE TASKS OF CONGRESS

Congress takes on nonlegislative tasks through special (or select) committees and joint committees. *Special, or select, committees*, unlike standing committees, are temporary committees and are established to examine specific issues. They must reestablish with each new Congress. *Joint committees* have members from both chambers, with the leadership alternating between Senate and House members. These committees investigate areas of concern, but they don't propose legislation.

The nonlegislative tasks of Congress include:

- **Oversight.** Congress oversees or reviews the work of the national government. It investigates charges of corruption and waste, and it holds hearings where experts and citizens discuss the government's problems and suggest solutions.
- Public Education. Committee hearings and floor debates increase public awareness of governmental and societal problems. Members of Congress take advantage of their *franking privilege*, which is the free use of the mail for official business, to send letters to their constituents (people whom they represent) that explain various problems and the proposed solutions.
- Helping Citizens Deal with Their Government. As representatives of their home constituents, members of Congress help citizens deal with the government. They listen to and act on complaints about the government and listen to suggestions about how to improve the government.

A Minute with Senator WordSmart
Set # 7

We learned about the nonlegislative work that Congress performs. This is Senator WordSmart's final set of words for this chapter.

1. Nonlegislative

2. Joint committee

3. Special, or Select, committee

a. Review of the work done by the national government.

b. Not associated with making laws.

c. Temporary committee within a chamber established to examine a specific issue.

4. Oversight

d. A temporary committee composed of members from the Senate and the House of Representatives.

5. Franking privilege

e. The free use of the mail for official congressional business.

As you can see, these tasks are important, but they can be time-consuming, as well. This chapter should have helped you appreciate the work that your Congress does. Maybe, in a few years, you would like to help with that work.

Projects You Can Do

1. The Senate and the House of Representatives each has a Web site that provides the addresses of every representative in Congress. Write to your senator or representative about some issue or problem that is important to you. Explain in the letter what you would like the senator or representative to do.
2. Ask an adult family member or your teacher to bring to class mail received from a congressperson. What are the subjects of the mailings?
3. Assume that you are a congressperson. Create your own mailing to your constituents that discusses a particular issue that interests you.

LET'S MEET THE PRESIDENT

Now that we have examined the legislative branch, let's take a look at another branch of the federal government: the executive branch.

CHAPTER FIVE

The Executive Branch

EXECUTIVE BRANCH

HOW THE EXECUTIVE BRANCH WAS CREATED

Along with the legislative branch, which we learned about in Chapter Four, and the judicial branch, which we'll read about in Chapter Six, the executive branch is one of the three branches of the federal government created by the Constitution. The *executive branch* is charged with executing or carrying out the laws of Congress, as well as representing the country when dealing with foreign countries. The *president*, who is also referred to as the chief executive, is the head of the executive branch. Initially, the writers of the Constitution had designed the other two branches to be equally important; however, because the president is the only nationally elected politician (along with the vice president), we see and hear more about the chief executive, especially in times of trouble. Therefore, the president, who lives and works at the White House in Washington, D.C., has become the most powerful figure in our government and the leader of our nation.

Under the *Articles of Confederation*, our country's first step toward a "constitution," there was no executive branch; Congress ran the national government, and the state legislatures governed their own states. Unfortunately, in the years immediately after the American Revolution, the Congress couldn't get much accomplished, and many state legislatures weren't doing much better. Both Congress and the state legislatures were having trouble passing laws and enforcing those they had passed because they lacked the authority and the people behind them to enforce the laws.

As this situation worsened, many Americans felt they needed a strong leader who not only could balance Congress's power to pass laws but also enforce the laws they had passed. They also wanted one person to represent them whom other countries would respect. Many, however, were afraid that creating a new leader might create a new king. Americans hardly wanted to jeopardize the rights and liberties they had fought so hard to win, and yet they had to do something because their new country was falling into chaos. Many realized the country needed a unified government that was located in one area, from which it could pass and enforce the laws that the whole country needed, rather than a governing group for each state. In other words, they wanted a *centralized government*. Also, they didn't want a leader who was involved with the politics of the Congress; rather, they wanted someone who represented *all* people. This meant that those wanting a strong leader and those wanting no leader needed to agree to some things that each side wanted in order to get the country on course. They needed to *compromise*—and they did.

The compromise created a presidency strong enough to match Congress, yet not so strong that it would overpower the legislative branch; the president was a leader with limited powers.

The delegates of the Constitutional Convention found some good ideas in New York's constitution, which empowered the New York voters, rather than the state legislature, to elect their *governor*, the chief executive of their state. New Yorkers elected their governor for a three-year term, and they didn't limit the number of terms that the governor could serve. Using New York as a guide, the delegates decided on a four-year term for the president, and the president, like the New York governor, could serve for an unlimited number of terms. (It wasn't until 1951, when Congress passed the Twenty-Second Amendment to the Constitution, that a president was limited to serve two successive four-year terms in office.)

ELECTION OF A PRESIDENT

Because the delegates wanted to elect the chief executive in a special way, they made another change to the New York method—Congress wouldn't elect the president, but neither would the citizen voters. Instead, a special body, the *electoral college*, would elect the president. Each state would have as many electors and *electoral votes* as it had senators and representatives. The Congress wanted the electors to be wise, politically experienced citizens who would apply their independent judgment. Unfortunately, the system didn't work like the delegates had intended because they didn't foresee the rise of political parties. Subsequently, the electors, rather than using their independent judgment, began voting for the candidate who belonged to the same party as they did. Soon, popular vote chose the electors, and all the electoral votes of a state went to the presidential candidate receiving the most votes in the state. (See Chapter Seven for more information on how we elect the president and members of Congress.) The table below lists the presidents, the years they served, and their political party.

President	Term	Political Party
1. George Washington	1789–1797	Federalist
2. John Adams	1797–1801	Federalist
3. Thomas Jefferson	1801–1809	Democratic-Republican
4. James Madison	1809–1817	Democratic-Republican
5. James Monroe	1817–1825	Democratic-Republican
6. John Quincy Adams	1825–1829	Democratic-Republican
7. Andrew Jackson	1829–1837	Democrat
8. Martin Van Buren	1837–1841	Democrat
9. William Harrison	1841	Whig
10. John Tyler	1841–1845	Whig
11. James Polk	1845–1849	Democrat
12. Zachary Taylor	1849–1850	Whig
13. Millard Fillmore	1850–1853	Whig
14. Franklin Pierce	1853–1857	Democrat
15. James Buchanan	1857–1861	Democrat
16. Abraham Lincoln	1861–1865	Republican
17. Andrew Johnson	1865–1869	Republican
18. Ulysses Grant	1869–1877	Republican

President	Term	Political Party
19. Rutherford Hayes	1877–1881	Republican
20. James Garfield	1881	Republican
21. Chester Arthur	1881–1885	Republican
22. Grover Cleveland	1885–1889	Democrat
23. Benjamin Harrison	1889–1893	Republican
24. Grover Cleveland	1893–1897	Democrat
25. William McKinley	1897–1901	Republican
26. Theodore Roosevelt	1901–1909	Republican
27. William Taft	1909–1913	Republican
28. Woodrow Wilson	1913–1921	Democrat
29. Warren Harding	1921–1923	Republican
30. Calvin Coolidge	1923–1929	Republican
31. Herbert Hoover	1929–1933	Republican
32. Franklin Roosevelt	1933–1945	Democrat
33. Harry Truman	1945–1953	Democrat
34. Dwight Eisenhower	1953–1961	Republican
35. John Kennedy	1961–1963	Democrat
36. Lyndon Johnson	1963–1969	Democrat
37. Richard Nixon	1969–1974	Republican
38. Gerald Ford	1974–1977	Republican
39. Jimmy Carter	1977–1981	Democrat
40. Ronald Reagan	1981–1989	Republican
41. George H. W. Bush	1989–1993	Republican
42. Bill Clinton	1993–2001	Democrat
43. George W. Bush	2001–	Republican

A Minute with Senator WordSmart

Set # 1

We've seen how the early Congress wrestled with creating an executive branch. Take a minute to make sure that you understand the meanings of the new words by matching the word in the left-hand column with its definition in the right-hand column by drawing a line from the word to its definition. If you want to check your work, review the Answer Key in the back of the book.

1. Executive branch

2. President

3. Compromise

4. Centralized government

5. Governor

6. Electoral college

7. Articles of Confederation

a. The body of people designated to elect the President.

b. The chief executive of the state.

c. The branch of government responsible for enforcing the laws passed by Congress and representing our country in dealing with foreign countries.

d. The "constitution" of the confederacy of the United States, written in 1777. The Constitution replaced these in 1788.

e. Reaching an agreement, by each side agreeing to some things the other side wants.

f. A form of government in which the national government governs from one central location.

g. The head of the executive branch, who is referred to as the Chief Executive.

As you might expect, the Constitutional Convention delegates didn't want just anyone elected president, so they decided that all presidential candidates should meet some minimum qualifications.

Minimum qualifications to be president

The delegates wrote the minimum qualifications to become president in Article II of the Constitution. At a minimum, anyone wanting to be the president must:

- have been born in the United States (The Constitution uses the term *natural-born citizen*). The only exception to this requirement is a person who was born in a foreign country, but to parents who are American citizens.
- be at least 35 years old.
- have lived in the United States for at least 14 years (but not necessarily the 14 years right before the election).

Did You Know?

The youngest president was John F. Kennedy. He was 42 years old when he was elected. The oldest president was Ronald Reagan, who was 77 years old when he left office.

JOHN F. KENNEDY

RONALD REAGAN

Surf's up...

Electing a president is one of our most important duties as citizens. Check out these sites to learn more:

bensguide.gpo.gov/6-8/election/general.html

vote-smart.org/reference/primer/pres.html

How much money does the president make?

Candidates run for president because they feel that they can be a good leader for our country. However, it is a still a job, therefore presidents are paid a salary and other benefits. The president earns:

- a salary of $400,000 a year
- a lifetime annual pension of $157,000 after leaving office.

Although people such as presidents of large companies, famous athletes, and movie stars make much more money, none have the powers and responsibilities of the president. Let's look at the power held by our chief executive.

The Choice Is Yours
Set # 1

To check your understanding of the previous material, answer the following questions by selecting the letter of the correct answer. If you want to check your work, refer to the Answer Key in the back of the book.

1. You must be at least _____ years old to run for president.
    a. 35
    b. 18
    c. 21
    d. 40

2. The chart below shows how long the following four presidents served in office. Which one served before Congress passed the Twenty-Second Amendment?

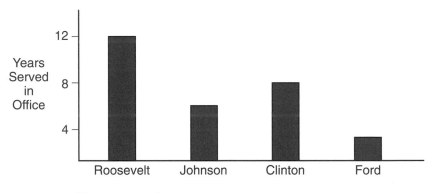

    a. Franklin Roosevelt
    b. Lyndon Johnson
    c. Bill Clinton
    d. Gerald Ford

3. The Confederation Congress used many of the ideas from
   _____ constitution to create the presidency.
   a. Pennsylvania's
   b. New York's
   c. Connecticut's
   d. Virginia's

4. Many Americans wanted to create a strong presidency because they wanted someone who could _____.
   a. balance the power of Congress
   b. enforce the laws passed by Congress
   c. represent them with foreign governments
   d. do all of the above

5. The chart below shows the salaries of four individuals. Which
   one could be president?

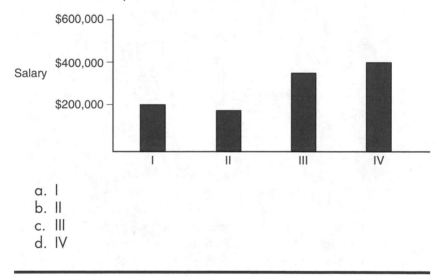

   a. I
   b. II
   c. III
   d. IV

Things to Think About

1. When he was president, Ronald Reagan wanted to repeal (abolish) the Twenty-Second Amendment. Do you think the president should be limited to two terms in office? Why or why not?

2. Would you add other minimum qualifications to become president? Why or why not? If so, what would they be?
3. Because of the electoral college, it's possible for a candidate who hasn't received the majority of the popular vote to be elected. Explain how this could happen.
4. What are the advantages and disadvantages of electing a president through the electoral college rather than through popular vote?
5. What other alternatives could the delegates have come up with besides a presidency and an executive branch?

POWERS OF THE PRESIDENT

Despite a certain dependence on Congress and the judiciary, the president emerged from the Constitutional Convention with strong powers; the Constitution granted some of these powers, but over time, presidents assumed others. First, let's look at the presidential powers that the Constitution grants.

Surf's up...

Cruise into this site and learn more about the president's constitutional powers:

vote-smart.org/reference/primer/pres.html

The enumerated powers

In contrast to the many powers the Constitution gives Congress, it grants fewer powers to the president. Most of **Article II** talks about the procedure for electing the president, the length of time the president can serve, qualifications for office, and procedures for succession and impeachment. Yet, specific powers were granted. We refer to these powers as the president's **enumerated powers**—that is, those powers specifically mentioned in the Constitution.

Article II, Section 2, states that the president shall have the power to do the following:

Command the armed forces

We refer to the president as the ***commander in chief*** of the armed forces because the president is the leader of the military. All officers in the armed forces ultimately report to the president. Although, as we read in Chapter Four, only Congress can declare war and approve funds for the military, the president has the final responsibility for conducting our country's military policy. Having the president as commander in chief ensures civilian control of the military forces, as the writers of the Constitution intended. They felt that a military-controlled Army and Navy could lead to a ***military dictatorship***, that is, control of the country by a single person who rules by the force of the military.

Commission (authorize) armed forces officers

As the commander in chief of the military, the president is empowered to commission (approve) the officers who will report and carry out the orders of the executive branch.

Pardon those guilty of some federal crimes

The president can grant reprieves (postpone punishment) and pardon (excuse) certain individuals convicted of federal crimes, except impeachment. ***Impeachment*** is the process of bringing charges against federal officials for wrongdoing. Granting reprieves and pardons is a tradition adopted from the Greeks and, more recently, from the British where the king showed mercy to certain deserving people who had been convicted of crimes.

The most famous recent reprieve occurred in 1974 when President Gerald Ford pardoned former President Richard Nixon for crimes that Nixon might have committed when he was president. He was able to do this because Richard Nixon resigned before Congress could bring impeachment charges.

Did You Know?

After he left the presidency, Richard Nixon gained praise for his accomplishments involving foreign leaders. By the time of his death in 1994, he had written numerous books on his experiences in public life and on foreign policy, especially his successes in opening relations with China and reducing tensions with our then Cold War enemy, the Soviet Union.

RICHARD M. NIXON

A Minute with Senator WordSmart
Set # 2

Match the word in the left-hand column with its definition in the right-hand column.

1. Natural-born citizen
2. Article II

3. Enumerated powers

4. Commander in chief

5. Military dictatorship

6. Impeach

a. The leader of the military.
b. The control of the country by a single person who rules by the force of the military.
c. To bring charges against federal officials for wrongdoing.
d. A person born in the country in which he or she is living.
e. The part of the Constitution that discusses the executive branch.
f. Those powers specifically mentioned in the Constitution.

Make treaties

The president is our chief diplomat. A diplomat is a person, such as an *ambassador*, who represents the country in relations with another country. The president and certain people on the president's staff work with leaders and diplomats representing other countries to make *treaties*, which are formal international agreements between the United States and a foreign country. According to Article II, for a treaty signed by the president to be valid, the Senate must approve it by a two-thirds vote.

Did You Know?

Most treaties are approved, but some are not. For instance, the Senate rejected the Treaty of Versailles (1919) that ended World War I and was signed by President Woodrow Wilson, because many senators felt that the treaty gave back too many rights and privileges to our wartime enemies.

Appoint ambassadors

As our country's chief diplomat, the president is in charge of appointing the ambassadors. Ambassadors are our country's representatives and are responsible for explaining American policy to other countries.

Many times, the president will appoint friends or people who have helped in the presidential campaign to these jobs. For instance, Roy Austin, our ambassador to Trinidad and Tobago, was a classmate of President Bush's at Yale University. The Constitution does limit this power because the Senate must approve all ambassadors and other diplomats that the president appoints.

Receive ambassadors and other public ministers

As the chief diplomat, the president spends considerable time hosting ambassadors at the White House for meetings and dinners. These meetings can result in historic decisions. For example, President Jimmy Carter personally worked out the Camp David Accords between Israel and Egypt in 1978, which led to a peace treaty between those two previously warring countries. For their efforts to resolve their long-standing conflict, Anwar al-Sadat, President of Egypt, and Menachem Begin, Prime Minister of Israel, jointly received the 1978 Nobel Peace Prize. Jimmy Carter was awarded the Nobel Peace Prize in 2002 as a tribute to his lifetime effort of trying to bring peace to hostile areas.

Appoint Supreme Court justices

The *Supreme Court* is the highest-ranking court in our country. We refer to the nine judges who make up the Supreme Court as *Supreme Court justices*. Supreme Court justices have unlimited terms. Most, in fact, retire from their work at an old age. (For more information about the Supreme Court, refer to Chapter Six.) When there is a vacancy in the Supreme Court, the president has the constitutional power to nominate (choose) a successor for the retiring justice; however, the Senate, by a two-thirds majority, must approve the president's nominees. (For more about the current Supreme Court justices, refer to Chapter Six.)

Appoint people to jobs within the federal government

Besides appointing Supreme Court justices and ambassadors, the president also has the power to appoint federal court judges, cabinet officers, and many other federal government positions.

The Constitution requires the advice and consent of the Senate for many of these appointments.

As an example, President George W. Bush recently appointed Tom Ridge, Secretary of Homeland Security. In fact, it was under President Bush's influence that both houses of Congress approved the Homeland Security Act of 2002, which created a federal department whose primary mission is to help prevent acts of terrorism on our soil. This legislation established a new executive department, the Office of Homeland Security.

Recommend legislation to Congress

Because the chief executive is the only nationally elected politician, the president serves as the representative for the entire country. In this role, the president is expected to propose legislation favored by a majority of the people. To do so, the president begins the administration's legislative agenda (program) with the *State of the Union Address*, which is a speech required by Article II to be given every January by the president to a joint session of Congress and to the American people. This speech sets out the president's proposals in domestic, foreign, and military affairs. These proposals become the agenda for the upcoming legislative session. Presidents follow their messages with drafts of legislation for certain representatives and senators to sponsor in Congress.

In our disillusionment after the last war, we preferred international anarchy to international cooperation with nations which did not see and think exactly as we did. We gave up the hope of gradually achieving a better peace because we had not the courage to fulfill our responsibilities in an admittedly imperfect world.

—President Franklin Roosevelt, 1945 State of the Union Address, given near the end of World War II

Shortly after the State of the Union Address, the president delivers another important message to Congress—the proposed budget. Under the Budget and Accounting Act of 1921, the president submits an *executive budget*, which is the president's proposed budget for the country, showing how much money the country will take in and how much it will spend. Once submitted, this budget goes to Congress for changes and approval.

The president and the president's aides can exert personal persuasion on key legislative members and negotiate compromises needed to advance the executive branch's proposed budget and legislation. For example, the executive branch can persuade legislators by promising that certain large government projects, particularly for defense and civil works construction, will go to those states whose legislators support the legislation. Typically, these contracts will be worth millions of dollars to the industries located in the legislator's home state.

As we saw in Chapter Three, Article I, Section 7, empowers the president through the power of the *veto* to reject legislation approved by both houses of Congress. If the president vetoes a bill, it takes a two-thirds vote of both houses (which is difficult to achieve) to accomplish a veto override. The president's veto power is an important check on the legislative power of Congress.

Did You Know?

Franklin D. Roosevelt leads all presidents in the number of presidential vetoes with 635.

From 1789 to present, there have been more than 1,400 presidential vetoes of proposed legislation; however, Congress has only managed to override a little more than 100.

Presidents can also use the threat of a veto to persuade Congress to make changes in bills they are considering passing. Similarly, the president can use the threat of a veto against a bill Congress wants badly in exchange for other bills that the president wants passed.

A Minute with Senator WordSmart
Set # 3

Match the word in the left-hand column with its definition in the right-hand column.

1. Ambassador

2. Treaty

3. Supreme Court

4. Supreme Court justices

5. State of the Union Address

6. Executive budget

7. Veto

a. The speech required by Article II to be given each January by the president to a joint session of Congress and the American people.

b. The judges who sit on the Supreme Court.

c. The highest ranking court in the United States.

d. A formal international agreement between two or more countries.

e. A person who represents the country in relations with another country.

f. The president's rejection of legislation approved by both houses of Congress.

g. The president's proposed budget for the country.

On occasion, convene one or both houses of Congress

During times of crisis, such as the threat of war, the president has the power to convene (call into session) one or both houses of Congress.

Did You Know?

Abraham Lincoln had to call a special session of Congress on July 4, 1861, to persuade them to pay for the war against the Confederacy.

ABRAHAM LINCOLN

The president also has the constitutional power to adjourn Congress (end the session) when the legislators can't agree on when to adjourn.

Enforce the laws that Congress has passed

The last sentence of Article II, Section 3, provides that the president "shall take care that the laws be faithfully executed." Remember that the writers of the Constitution wanted the president to enforce the laws that Congress passed. In part, the president does this by appointing the attorney general. The *attorney general* heads the Department of Justice, making that person the chief law enforcement officer in the country. The attorney general reports to the president on the success or failure of enforcing the laws.

The Choice Is Yours
Set # 2

To check your understanding of the previous material, answer the following questions by selecting the letter of the correct answer.

1. The following is not a constitutionally enumerated power of the president:
   a. Appoint Supreme Court justices when a vacancy occurs
   b. Veto legislation
   c. Introduce legislation
   d. Appoint ambassadors

2. The president usually appoints _____ to ambassador positions.
   a. college professors
   b. friends and people who helped with the campaign
   c. people selected by the other countries
   d. military officers

3. The president may grant reprieves and pardons to certain individuals convicted of _____.
   a. murder
   b. shoplifting
   c. federal crimes
   d. speeding

4. Which of the events along the time line involved president George H. Bush (the father of our current president)?

```
                Treaty of                              Camp David
                Versailles                              Accords      NAFTA
                   ↓                                       ↓           ↓
   ┬──────┬──────┬──────┬──────┬──────┬──────┬──────┬──────┬──────┬
  1900   1910   1920   1930   1940   1950   1960   1970   1980   1990   2000
```

   a. Camp David Accords
   b. North American Free Trade Agreement (NAFTA)
   c. Treaty of Versailles
   d. None of the above

5. Once the president vetoes a bill, it takes _____ of both chambers of Congress to override the veto.
   a. 100 percent
   b. 50 percent
   c. 66 percent
   d. 75 percent

We've looked at the powers the Constitution has given the president; however, the president has come to have additional powers. We refer to these powers, which derive from the enumerated powers, as the president's inherent powers.

The inherent powers

From the moment George Washington took office, presidential authority has increased because every president has taken advantage of the inherent powers of the presidency. *Inherent powers* are those powers that the president exercises in *foreign affairs* (interactions with other countries) that aren't written in our Constitution, but are necessary to keep the national government functioning. Why has this happened? Presidents consider themselves representatives of all people; therefore, they believe they have the right to pursue the desires of the people by using whatever powers they can until another branch of government limits that power.

For example, as commanders in chief of the armed forces, presidents have ordered American troops into combat without congressional authorization. The most famous example was when President Johnson sent additional troops into the Vietnam War without consulting Congress. Other examples don't involve military conflict. To avoid obtaining congressional approval, presidents have signed executive agreements with foreign countries. *Executive agreements* function nearly the same as treaties, but the president doesn't need approval from two-thirds of the Senate. When some members of Congress challenged the legality of these agreements, the Supreme Court ruled that they were within the inherent powers of the president.

The North American Free Trade Agreement (NAFTA) is a recent example of an executive agreement (although both the Senate and the House approved it, but only by a majority vote). This agreement, signed by President George H. Bush in 1992, gradually removed tariffs and other trade barriers on most goods produced and sold in North America.

Did You Know?

Early in the 1800s, President Thomas Jefferson made one of the first executive agreements. As war raged through Europe and on the Atlantic Ocean between Great Britain and France, President Jefferson agreed to remain neutral.

The Choice Is Yours
Set # 3

To check your understanding of the previous material, answer the following questions by selecting the letter of the correct answer.

1. The president enforces the laws of Congress through the appointment of the _____.
   a. vice president
   b. attorney general
   c. ambassador to France
   d. Supreme Court justices

2. The president uses the _____ as a plan for the upcoming year's legislation.
   a. State of the Union Address
   b. executive budget
   c. veto power
   d. all of the above

3. Most of the president's inherent powers occur in the area of _____.
   a. the economy
   b. the federal courts
   c. vetoing legislation
   d. foreign affairs

4. _____ are much like treaties, except they don't need approval from two-thirds of the Senate to become valid.
   a. Bills
   b. Executive agreements
   c. Budgets
   d. None of the above

5. Presidents consider themselves _____.
   a. representatives of all people
   b. above the law
   c. the leaders of the judicial branch
   d. the spokesperson for their state

Additional powers granted by Congress

Although the president's enumerated constitutional powers have remained unchanged over the years, the total power of the office has increased, not only because presidents have expanded their inherent powers but also because they have taken legislative action. Expanding inherent powers have given the president more powers in foreign affairs, while Congress has given additional powers to the executive branch in the area of domestic policy. Congress has created new departments and agencies that have given the president and the executive branch broad powers to tackle problems related to education, poverty, and the environment. The trend throughout the twentieth century has been to increase presidential powers at the expense of Congress because it seems the voters feel more confident that the president can solve problems better and more quickly than Congress.

An example of this increased presidential power is the executive order. The president issues an *executive order* in order to interpret or carry out a law. The Constitution doesn't mention executive orders anywhere, yet they are accepted as legal authority. Executive orders are essential because Congress, although it has the right to do so, often doesn't spell out how a law it has just passed should work or be implemented. For a number of reasons, Congress leaves this to the president. Executive orders cover various subjects. Some recent examples of executive orders issued by President Bush are:

- He created a Board of Inquiry to help settle the dock workers strike on the Pacific Coast.
- He expanded the role of the President's Council on Physical Fitness and Sports.
- He set up guidelines for colleges and universities that serve Native Americans.

Did You Know?

Ronald Reagan believed in a strong presidency. He issued more than 400 executive orders.

Personal influence

Presidents also have not hesitated to use the personal power of the office to influence events. For example, during the crippling coal strike in winter 1902, President Theodore Roosevelt invited both labor and mine owners to the White House so that they could settle the strike. Roosevelt had no legal power to settle the strike; he assumed his influence would make the sides settle (which they did). Some 60 years later, President Kennedy criticized the steel manufacturers for raising the price of steel by saying that increased prices would bring hardship to the country; the steel companies lowered the price back to where they had been.

Projects You Can Do

Use your local public library or the Internet to:

1. Select a president with whom you are unfamiliar. Find out:
   - what important events occurred during his term
   - what legislation and policies were passed during his term.

2. Learn about our president's last trip to a foreign country. Where did he go? What did he discuss?

3. What were the issues and problems that faced George Washington? What issues and problems face our current president?

Limitation of the president's power

As we have seen, the writers of the Constitution recognized the need for a system of *checks and balances*—that is, an arrangement of governmental powers where powers of one government branch limit those of the other branches. They incorporated these checks and balances into the Constitution. With the steady increase of power to the executive branch, it is even more important for our system of government to have checks and balances, especially ways to limit presidential power. Examples of the Constitution's checks on the president's power include the following:

- The president is subject to a congressional override of his veto.
- The president needs two-thirds of the Senate to approve treaties and appointments.
- The judicial branch has the power to review the president's actions and declare them unconstitutional—that is, not permitted by the Constitution.
- The president serves only a four-year term and has been limited to two consecutive terms since the Twenty-Second Amendment won approval in 1951.

Things to Think About

1. Discuss the advantages and disadvantages of the president receiving additional powers not mentioned in the Constitution.
2. Do executive agreements go against the intentions of the writers of the Constitution?

Beside limits placed on the president's power by checks and balances established in the Constitution, the *media* (newspapers, magazines, radio, television, and the Internet) also limits the president's power because it is continuously reporting on and investigating the president. This constant scrutiny keeps the public informed of the president's actions so that the president can't overstep the branch's power in a secretive way. (For more information on the effect of the media on government policy, see Chapter Eight.)

The Choice Is Yours
Set # 4

To check your understanding of the previous material, answer the following questions by selecting the letter of the correct answer.

1. The chart below shows the number of senators who approved various treaties that the president signed. Which treaty is valid?

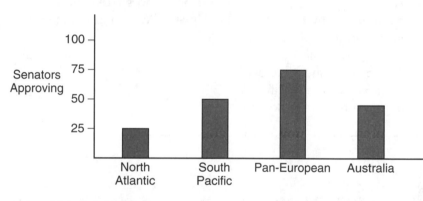

a. North Atlantic Treaty
b. South Pacific Treaty
c. Pan-European Treaty
d. Australia Treaty

2. Over the years, presidential power has increased through
_____.
a. exercise of inherent powers
b. legislative action
c. the use of the military
d. a and b

3. The president's formal constitutional power has changed little over the years.
   a. True
   b. False
   c. Hard to tell
   d. The Constitution does not grant powers to the president

4. The trend throughout the twentieth century has been to increase presidential powers at the expense of _____.
   a. the American people
   b. the judiciary
   c. the states
   d. Congress

5. As the _____, the president represents and speaks for the country, both when he is in the United States and when he is in a foreign country.
   a. chief executive officer
   b. leader of the judiciary
   c. most popular politician
   d. governor of his home state

We have the power

The most effective way to keep the president from taking too much power is to communicate with our representatives and vote. Active citizen participation in government can and does make a difference. Because they must compete in nationwide elections, presidents listen to public opinion everywhere. Even when the president isn't up for reelection, citizens can express their displeasure with the president's actions by changing parties, voting out members of Congress who agree with the president's actions, and organizing protests. Although they didn't mention it in the Constitution, the writers knew that citizen dissatisfaction with government can change a president's policies and can keep the president from being reelected. Because this process may take a few years, they did provide an immediate solution if the president abused the power of the office and committed criminal acts. In that case, the Constitution provides a procedure for the impeachment and removal of the president from office.

REMOVAL OF THE PRESIDENT

Article II, Section 4, establishes the process to *impeach* (bring charges against for wrongdoing) and remove the president for "Treason, Bribery, or other Crimes and Misdemeanors." The Constitution places the power to impeach the president in the most politically responsive body of the government—the House of Representatives. The writers did this because they felt that removing a president from office should reflect the will of citizens, just as electing a president to office does. Because removing a president is such a serious matter, the Constitution requires that the desire to do so must be overwhelming. Let's look at how the process works:

Step One: A majority of the members of the House of Representatives must vote to impeach.

Step Two: Once the House votes to impeach, the Senate then conducts the trial of the president. The Chief Justice of the Supreme Court presides over (directs) the trial.

Step Three: At the conclusion of the trial, each senator votes.

Step Four: If the Senate acquits the president, meaning that more than one-third of the senators vote that the president is "not guilty," the president may continue to serve. If the Senate finds the president "guilty," the vice president (assuming the vice president isn't also being removed from office) becomes the president.

Did You Know?

The House of Representatives has impeached only two presidents: Andrew Johnson in 1868 and Bill Clinton in 1999. The Senate, however, didn't remove either from office.

Richard Nixon resigned when it became apparent that Congress would impeach and likely convict him for his role in the Watergate scandal.

Originally, the Constitution didn't address what to do when the vice president replaces the president. As a result, some vice presidents who became presidents served without vice presidents. For example, after John F. Kennedy was assassinated, Lyndon Johnson served a year without a vice president. Consequently, in 1967, Congress passed the Twenty-Fifth Amendment to take care of this problem. Under this amendment, the new president nominates (chooses) a vice president, who then must be confirmed (approved) by a majority in both houses of Congress. The president and Congress followed this process twice in the 1970s—first, when Gerald Ford became vice president after Vice President Spiro Agnew resigned and again when President Ford appointed Nelson Rockefeller as his vice president after President Nixon resigned.

Similarly, the original Constitution had no provision for declaring the president disabled—that is, either physically or mentally unable to carry out the duties of the presidency. Congress also addressed this situation when they passed the Twenty-Fifth Amendment, which, along with dealing with selecting a new vice president also included provisions for determining disability, transferring power to the vice president, and discussing how a disabled president may regain power.

A Minute with Senator WordSmart
Set # 4

Match the word in the left-hand column with its definition in the right-hand column.

1. Inherent powers

    a. An arrangement of governmental powers where powers of one government branch limits those of the other branches.

2. Foreign affairs

    b. Interactions with other countries.

3. Executive agreement

    c. Writing issued by the president that interprets or implements a law.

4. Executive order

    d. A treaty-like agreement with another country signed by the president, but not approved by two-thirds of the Senate.

5. Checks and balances

    e. Those powers exercised by the president in foreign affairs that aren't mentioned in the Constitution but are necessary to keep the national government functioning.

6. Media

    f. Newspapers, magazines, radio, television, and the Internet.

THE LINE OF SUCCESSION TO THE PRESIDENCY

As we have seen, if the Senate removes the president from office or if the president dies, resigns, or is unable to carry out the duties of the office, the vice president will replace the president. What if the vice president is not available? Who then becomes president? After all, the orderly transition of power in the executive branch is necessary to the stability of our constitutional government.

To provide that stability, Congress has passed the Presidential Succession Act of 1947. (The act has been amended as new executive agencies have been added, establishing the line of succession after the vice president, which is shown below.) Each person in the line is a member of the cabinet. No, the cabinet is not a piece of furniture in the White House! It is a group of the president's advisors. (Refer to the next section on executive bureaucracy to learn more about the president's cabinet.) The cabinet member's place in line is determined by when the department was established; the earlier Congress established the department, the higher up the succession ladder the department's head is. However, the constitutional qualifications still apply. For example, if the secretary of state had been born in a foreign country to parents who were not U.S. citizens, that person would be bypassed in this line.

Line of Succession to the Presidency

1. Vice President
2. Speaker of the House
3. Senate President Pro Tempore
4. Secretary of State
5. Secretary of the Treasury
6. Secretary of Defense
7. Attorney General
8. Secretary of Interior
9. Secretary of Agriculture
10. Secretary of Commerce
11. Secretary of Labor

12. Secretary of Health and Human Resources
13. Secretary of Housing and Urban Development
14. Secretary of Transportation
15. Secretary of Energy
16. Secretary of Education
17. Secretary of Veterans Affairs
18. Secretary of Homeland Security

Surf's up...

This site tells you more about the line to the presidency:

usconstitution.net/consttop_succ.html

Did You Know?

In 1849, president-elect Zachary Taylor, a devout Episcopalian, refused to take the oath of office on a Sunday, which is considered a day of rest in his religion. Consequently, the ceremony was postponed until noon on Monday, March 5. In the meantime, the country was without a president; James Polk and his vice president, George Dallas, had already resigned. By rules of succession at the time, the next person in line was the president pro tempore of the Senate, David Atchison. Although history doesn't record it this way, many historians feel that Atchison was president for a day, making him our twelfth president.

Projects You Can Do

Use the Internet or your local public library to:

1. Construct a diagram of the checks and balances in our federal government.
2. Compare the president's cabinet with the Prime Minister of Great Britain's advisors.
3. Learn how the media has limited the power of a president in a particular situation. Describe the situation. How was the president's power limited?

THE VICE PRESIDENT

Under the Constitution, the vice president serves as the president of the Senate (but voting only to break ties) and succeeds the president in the event of death, resignation, or a disability, such as a stroke or emotional illness. Consequently, many people refer to the vice president as "being a heartbeat away from the presidency." Indeed, seven vice presidents have had to assume the presidency:

- John Tyler replaced William Harrison, who died of pneumonia after serving just 1 month.
- Millard Fillmore replaced Zachary Taylor, who died after serving a little more than 18 months.
- Andrew Johnson replaced Abraham Lincoln, who was shot and killed by John Wilkes Booth.
- Chester Arthur replaced James Garfield, who died 11 weeks after an assassin shot him.
- Theodore Roosevelt replaced William McKinley, who died 8 days after being shot by an assassin at the Pan-American Exposition.
- Calvin Coolidge replaced Warren Harding, who died after returning from a trip to Alaska.
- Lyndon Johnson replaced John Kennedy, who was assassinated by Lee Harvey Oswald in 1963.

Until the last 2 decades, most presidential candidates selected their running mates based more on the voters they might attract rather than their skills to carry out the job as president if the job were suddenly thrust on them. Ronald Reagan, because of his advanced age (he was 69 years old when he took office in 1984), was the first modern president to select his running mate, George H. Bush, based on his leadership skills. Subsequently, Bill Clinton and George W. Bush chose their vice presidents more for their leadership abilities rather than their vote-getting appeal.

The Choice Is Yours
Set # 5

To check your understanding of the previous material, answer the following questions by selecting the letter of the correct answer.

1. It wasn't until Congress passed the _____ that it addressed the problem of selecting another vice president when the current vice president had to replace the president.
   a. Elastic Clause
   b. Bill of Rights
   c. Twenty-Fifth Amendment
   d. Twenty-Second Amendment

2. The following is the correct line of succession to the presidency:
   a. Secretary of commerce, vice president, Speaker of the House
   b. Vice president, Speaker of the House, Senate president pro tempore
   c. Vice president, Senate president pro tempore, Speaker of the House
   d. Speaker of the House, vice president, secretary of state

3. _____ vice presidents have become president because the previous president died in office.
   a. Zero
   b. Four
   c. Fifteen
   d. Seven

4. The chart below shows the number of senators voting to remove the president from office after four separate impeachment proceedings. Which president(s) should be removed from office?

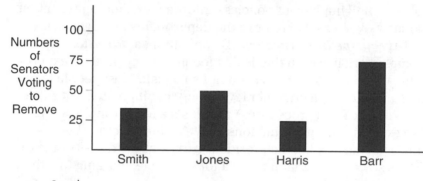

   a. Smith
   b. Jones
   c. Harris
   d. Barr

5. The most effective way to keep the president from taking too much power is _____.
   a. elect weak presidents
   b. for citizens to participate actively in our government
   c. don't vote for a president
   d. elect a popular vice president

THE EXECUTIVE BUREAUCRACY

As the powers and responsibilities of the presidency increase, the president doesn't have time to do all the work that the job now requires, so presidents must rely on aides, advisors, and entire agencies for help. The vast executive branch, which is organized into more than one-hundred departments, agencies, boards, and commissions, contains more than three million employees. The people in these various departments help the president schedule appointments, communicate with legislators, develop and implement policies, enforce laws, and represent our country overseas. We refer to the departments and agencies as the *executive bureaucracy*. By definition, a *bureaucracy* is a complex organization that is divided into many parts or experts, who, together, all work to accomplish a task. Most people have a negative view of a bureaucracy, saying that it creates *red tape* (lots of rules and procedures) and costs a lot to run. However, the executive branch functions best as a bureaucracy because advising and helping the president carry out the duties of the office is so complex that it takes a lot of people, working together, to accomplish it.

Did You Know?

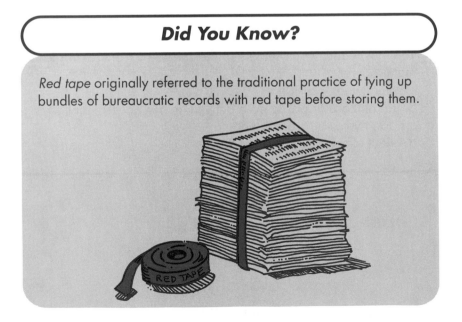

Red tape originally referred to the traditional practice of tying up bundles of bureaucratic records with red tape before storing them.

The executive bureaucracy, led by the president, is divided into three main parts:

1. White House Office Staff
2. Executive Office of the President
3. Cabinet.

The White House office staff

The ***White House Office Staff*** consists of about 500 aides and advisors who help the president with daily affairs. Aside from advising the president on various policy areas, these aides and advisors help the president with everything from scheduling appointments to public relations. Thus, the staff must include press and appointment secretaries, various administrative assistants, and many office workers.

Surf's up...

There is much to learn about the executive bureaucracy. This site will help you out:

vote-smart.org/official_president.php

Executive office of the president

The *Executive Office of the President*, established in 1939, contains about 15 staff agencies that help the president. Of the 15 agencies, the 3 most important are:

- *Office of Management and Budget (OMB)*
  The OMB advises the president regarding the budget and operations of the hundreds of government departments and agencies. This agency prepares and oversees the executive budget and evaluates agency programs.
- *Council of Economic Advisors*
  The Employment Act of 1946 created the Council of Economic Advisors. This agency helps the president prepare the annual economic report to Congress and undertakes special studies for the president.
- *National Security Council (NSC)*
  The NSC was created in 1947. It helps develop policy for national security and foreign affairs. By law, the president, the vice president, the secretary of state, and the secretary of defense belong to the agency. The president, who presides, may invite other agency heads to attend the NSC's meetings.

The cabinet

You can read all through the Constitution, and you won't find anything about how the executive branch should be organized, other than mentioning "executive departments." These became the basis for the *cabinet*, which is a multiagency advisory council to the president. The modern-day cabinet consists of the president, the vice president, and the heads of 15 executive agencies. Since the creation of the NSC, the cabinet concentrates on domestic and political matters.

Although the Constitution didn't mention the cabinet and who should be in it, every president has had one. George Washington created the first cabinet in 1789. It consisted of people who headed the following four agencies:

Agency	Cabinet Member
Department of Justice	Attorney general
State Department	Secretary of state
Treasury	Secretary of the treasury
War	Secretary of war

As the federal government grew, the number of executive agencies increased. The table below shows the departments represented in the cabinet and the year they were established. Each of the cabinet members have the title of *Secretary*, except for the head of the Department of Justice, who is referred to as the **attorney general**. Selecting the cabinet is the first major job for the president-elect.

Cabinet departments and year of establishment

Justice (1789)	State (1789)
Treasury (1789)	Interior (1849)
Agriculture (1889)	Commerce (1903)
Labor (1913)	Defense (1947)
Health and Human Services (1953)	Housing and Urban Development (1965)
Transportation (1967)	Energy (1977)
Education (1979)	Veterans' Affairs (1989)
Homeland Security (2002)	

A Minute with Senator WordSmart
Set # 5

Match the word in the left-hand column with its definition in the right-hand column.

1. Executive bureaucracy

2. White House Office Staff

3. Executive Office of the President

4. Office of Management and Budget (OMB)
5. Council of Economic Advisors
6. National Security Council (NSC)

a. Contains 15 staff agencies, including the Office of Management and Budget, the Council of Economic Advisors, and the National Security Council.

b. Advisory council to the president that consists of the president, vice president, and heads of 15 executive agencies.

c. Three million people who help the president. Divided into three parts: White House Office Staff, Executive Office of the President, and the Cabinet.

d. Develops policy for national security and foreign affairs.

e. Head of the Department of Justice.

f. Advises the president regarding the budget and operation of government departments and agencies.

7. Cabinet

g. 500 aides and advisors who help the president with daily affairs.

8. Attorney general

h. Helps the president prepare the annual economic report to Congress.

Projects You Can Do

Use your local public library or the Internet to:

1. Learn more about one of the vice presidents who became president.
2. Research one cabinet department, such as the Department of Labor. Discuss the department's powers and responsibilities.
3. Learn more about one of the three main staff agencies in the Executive Office of the President: the Office of Management and Budget, the Council of Economic Advisors, or the National Security Council. What is that agency's responsibility?

We've learned about the presidency and the executive branch. Now let's find out about the judicial branch.

CHAPTER SIX

The Judicial Branch

HOW THE JUDICIAL BRANCH WAS CREATED

The judicial branch, the legislative branch, and the executive branch comprise the three branches of the federal government. The word *judicial* means, "relating to laws and courts." Consequently, the *judicial branch* interprets the laws and establishes the procedures to apply them through the court system.

As the Constitution's writers intended, by effectively interpreting and guarding our laws, the judicial branch enables our country to be ruled by laws rather than by the whims of powerful people. Because ours is a country ruled by laws administered through the judicial process, we should be able to settle disputes fairly and peacefully.

THE JUDICIAL PROCESS

During medieval times, subjects would travel to the king's court so that he could settle their disputes. We don't have a king, but we still have courts. In our *courts*, judges, lawyers, and juries come together to help their fellow citizens peacefully settle disputes through the *judicial process* we refer to as a trial. A *trial* is a legal examination in which the disputing groups of people meet in a court and present their positions to an impartial decision maker. The *defendant* (the person accused of the wrongdoing or crime) and the *plaintiff* (the person or the designated government official accusing the defendant) present *evidence* (facts that support their position) so that a judge or a *jury* (a group of citizens not involved with the dispute) can decide the outcome of the dispute. Once both sides have presented their evidence, the judge or the jury decides in favor of either the defendant or the plaintiff. We refer to a dispute that has been brought into a court as a *case*. There are two kinds of cases in our judicial process:

- *Criminal law cases*
  These are disputes in which the government charges an
  individual with committing a crime and violating a law that
  protects another person's safety. Examples of such criminal
  acts are burglary and murder. A person convicted of committing a criminal act may be sent to jail as punishment.
- *Civil law cases*
  These are disputes among individual citizens or individual citizens and government officials over property or money. Unlike
  criminal law cases, the defendant isn't being accused of committing a crime, so the punishment is usually paying money,
  not going to jail.

Surf's up...

Check out these sites to learn
more about the judicial branch
and process:

socialstudieshelp.com/Lesson_13_Notes.htm

congressforkids.net/judicialbranch.htm

A Minute with Senator WordSmart

Set # 1

Take a minute to make sure that you under-stand the meanings of the new words. Match the word in the left-hand column with its defi-nition in the right-hand column by drawing a line from the word to its definition. If you want to check your work, review the Answer Key in the back of the book.

1. Judicial

2. Judicial branch

3. Court
4. Plaintiff

5. Evidence

6. Jury

7. Judicial process

8. Trial

9. Defendant

a. Branch of the government that interprets laws.

b. Disputes where a designated government official charges an individual with violating a law that protects another person's safety. Such cases involve a crime, such as burglary or murder.

c. Relating to laws and courts.

d. A dispute that has been brought into a court.

e. A place where we peacefully settle disputes.

f. A process of examination in a court to peacefully settle a dispute.

g. Involves two groups of people coming together in a court and presenting their positions in the case to a decision maker.

h. Disputes among individual citizens or individual citizens and a designated government official over property or money.

i. Group of citizens not involved in the dispute who have the responsibility to decide the outcome of the dispute.

10. Case

11. Criminal law cases

12. Civil law cases

j. The party who accuses the other party of wrongdoing.

k. Facts that support a person's position in a court case.

l. The person accused of wrongdoing.

The Choice Is Yours
Set # 1

To check your understanding of the previous material, answer the following questions by selecting the letter of the correct answer. If you want to check your work, refer to the Answer Key in the back of the book.

1. The responsibility of the judicial branch is to _____.
   a. enforce the laws
   b. create the laws
   c. interpret the laws
   d. do all of the above

2. An example of a criminal case is _____.
   a. burglary of a home
   b. a dispute over the wording in a contract
   c. a dispute over the sale of some land
   d. b and c

3. In the United States, we settle our disputes peacefully in _____.
   a. auditoriums
   b. courts
   c. restaurants
   d. schools

4. The person accused of a crime is referred to as the _____.
   a. plaintiff
   b. defendant
   c. lawyer
   d. judge

5. _____ is presented at trials to persuade the judge or jury.
   a. Money
   b. Evidence
   c. Trivia
   d. A mathematic equation

Projects You Can Do

1. Watch a courtroom show on television. Identify the:

   - plaintiff
   - defendant
   - judge
   - lawyers
   - jury

   What type of case was it? What was the outcome of the trial?
2. Ask your teacher if your class can sit in on a trial. How is a real trial different from a television trial? How is it the same?
3. Learn about the training that lawyers receive so they can represent people in court.

To make settling disputes more available to all people, the courts in the United States are organized into two systems. One court system serves on the state level, whereas the other serves on the national or federal level. Although both settle different types of disputes, the two systems, ultimately, work together.

THE STATE COURT SYSTEM

Each state has its own court system that settles disputes involving its own state laws. *State laws* are enacted by a state's legislature and apply to people living in or visiting that state. In contrast, *federal laws* are enacted by the U.S. Congress and apply to all people, regardless of the state in which they live. Although these state court systems are separate from the judicial branch, they ultimately come under its authority because lawyers may challenge some of the procedures and decisions in the state courts as being *unconstitutional* (violating the guidelines of the Constitution). First, let's look at the state court system, and then we'll see how it interacts with the judicial branch.

The *state court system* is organized into three levels of authority:

- superior or district courts
- state courts of appeals
- state supreme court.

Superior or district courts are trial courts that handle cases throughout the state. If the defendant loses the trial and there are questions about certain legal procedures that occurred during the trial, the defendant may appeal the case. An *appeal* is a request for review of the court's decision by a *state court of appeals*. States organize their courts of appeals by region, and each region handles the appeals of all district courts in its region. For example, Texas has 14 courts of appeals that handle appeals from district courts all over the state. Here, the defendant's lawyer presents the case to a panel (group) of judges (usually three), rather than a jury or a single judge, as in the trial court. The panel reaches their decision by a majority vote. The court of appeals can either:

- agree with the lower court's decision
- disagree and overrule the lower court's decision
- order a new trial in the lower court.

The judicial process is an important heritage of our country. Without it we would live in an environment of violence and oppression, rather than a society that values laws and fairness.

Surf's up...

Coast into these sites to learn more about the state court system:

courts.state.tx.us/publicinfo/crt_stru.htm

weblocator.com/attorney/tx/law.html

Of the many cases heard by the trial courts throughout each state, only a small percentage moves on to the state appeals courts. In certain instances, a defendant can appeal a state court's decision to a federal court if the defendant can convince the federal court that some of the procedures the state court used while hearing the case violated that person's constitutional rights.

Depending on the facts related to a case decided in a court of appeals, the losing party may want the *state supreme court* to review the case. The state supreme court is the highest court of authority in the state court system. As with the courts of appeals, state supreme court justices sit in panels when hearing cases. The decision of the state supreme court justices in the case becomes final unless the losing party can convince the Supreme Court to review the case. We'll see later how the Supreme Court decides to review a state supreme court case.

A Minute with Senator WordSmart
Set # 2

Take a minute to make sure that you understand the meanings of the new words. Match
the word in the left-hand column with its definition in the right-hand column.

1. State laws

2. Federal laws

3. Unconstitutional

4. State court system

5. Superior or district courts

6. State courts of appeals

7. State supreme court

a. Laws enacted by Congress that
apply to all people, regardless
of the state in which they live.

b. Trial courts that handle cases
throughout the state.

c. The highest court of authority in
the state.

d. System of courts consisting of
district courts, courts of appeal,
and a supreme court.

e. Laws enacted by a state's
legislature and applied to
people living in or visiting the
state.

f. State courts with the authority to
review state district court
decisions.

g. Violating the guidelines of the
Constitution.

Did You Know?

With its 1810 decision in *Fletcher v. Peck*, the Supreme Court, for
the first time, declared a state law unconstitutional.

The Choice Is Yours
Set # 2

To check your understanding of the previous material, answer the following questions by selecting the letter of the correct answer.

1. The order of courts in the state court system from lowest authority to highest authority is _____.
   a. state supreme court, district courts, state courts of appeals
   b. district courts, state courts of appeals, state supreme court
   c. state courts of appeals, district courts, state supreme court
   d. all the state courts are equal in authority

2. The state supreme court justices sit _____ to hear cases.
   a. by themselves
   b. with courts of appeals judges
   c. in panels of judges
   d. none of the above

3. A verdict of a state superior or district-level court can be reversed by _____.
   a. Congress
   b. a state court of appeals
   c. the governor
   d. the state legislature

4. The states organize their courts of appeals by _____.
   a. alphabetical order
   b. importance
   c. regions
   d. closeness to big cities

5. State superior or district-level courts are _____ courts.
   a. secret
   b. criminal
   c. appeals
   d. trial

Projects You Can Do

Use the Internet or your local public library to:

1. Determine the state district court and the court of appeals that have jurisdiction (authority to hear cases) over the city in which you live.
2. Learn about your state's courts of appeals. How many courts are there? How many cases do they hear each year?
3. Learn the qualifications to be a judge on your state's supreme court. Where is your state's supreme court located? How many judges sit on the court?

THE STRUCTURE OF THE JUDICIAL BRANCH

The writers of the Constitution established the most important part of the judicial branch in Article III, Section 1, when they created the *Supreme Court* to be the court of highest authority in our country.

Article III, Section 1 provides that:

> The judicial Power of the United States shall be vested in one supreme Court, and in such inferior Courts as Congress may from time to time ordain and establish.

With the exception of the Supreme Court, the Constitution left the task of developing the judicial branch to Congress. Congress accomplished this task by enacting the *Judiciary Act of 1789*, which created the federal district courts and the circuit courts of appeals (the "inferior Courts" mentioned in Article III). The *judicial branch* has the authority to hear cases involving federal (national) laws or cases from state courts involving an interpretation of the Constitution.

Federal district courts

There are 94 federal district courts: 89 in the 50 states, plus 1 in the District of Columbia, 1 in Puerto Rico, and 3 territorial courts. More than 600 permanent judges handle the cases that come to these courts. (Congress has the right to add temporary judges if the caseload requires.) The *federal district courts* are trial courts that hear both civil and criminal cases relating to federal laws. These courts have *jurisdiction* (authority to hear cases) over such federal crimes as:

- mail fraud (using the mail to cheat people out of their money)

- counterfeiting (making fake money)

- smuggling (illegally taking goods in or out of a state without paying the required taxes on them)
- bank robbery
- illegal interstate commerce (the illegal buying and selling of goods between citizens living in different states).

In some instances, federal district courts also serve as appeals courts to review state trial court cases where the defendant claims that procedures used during the trial violated that person's rights under the Constitution.

Each federal district court takes care of a specific geographic area in the nation. There is at least one district court in each state, and some states have as many as four district courts. Each federal district court has from 2 to 28 judges (all have been appointed by a president for a life term), depending on the number of cases within the district.

Compared with the state trial courts where juries decide most of the cases, juries decide about only half the cases in federal district courts.

Surf's up...

To find out more about the inferior courts of the judicial branch, check out these web sites:

polisci.com/almanac/judicial/usdcts.htm

uscourts.gov.courtofappeals.html

Federal circuit courts of appeals

Some cases decided in federal district courts are eligible for review in the *federal circuit courts of appeals*, which are the appeals courts with authority over the federal district courts. The United States divides itself into twelve judicial *circuits* or geographic areas, each circuit with one court of appeals. The District of Columbia has its own circuit court. Eleven of the circuits cover several states (see MAP on page 177). The Ninth Circuit goes outside of the United States by taking in Alaska, Hawaii, six western states, Guam, and the Northern Mariana Islands. By contrast, the Fifth Circuit covers only three states (Texas, Louisiana, and Mississippi). There are 179 courts of appeals judges.

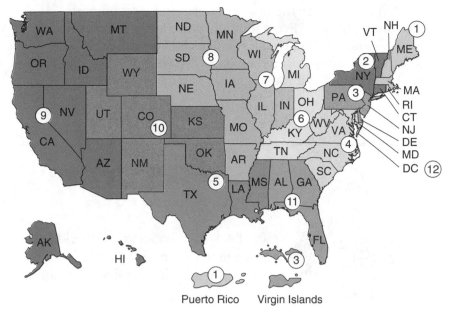

The U.S. Court of Appeals
SOURCE: *The Federal Register*.

Federal court judges

Each circuit court of appeals has from 6 to 28 permanent judges, depending on the number of cases in the circuit. As with the district courts, Congress has the right to add temporary judges. Each circuit court normally hears cases in panels of three judges; however, all the judges may decide to sit together to hear an important case.

Judges sitting in the district courts and circuit courts of appeal are required to live within the geographic boundaries of their courts. Although federal judges are appointed for a life term, they may be impeached (charged with a crime) and removed from office if found guilty of charges of wrongdoing.

The Choice Is Yours
Set # 3

To check your understanding of the previous material, answer the following questions by selecting the letter of the correct answer.

1. _____ of the Constitution established the Supreme Court.
   a. Article II, Section 1
   b. Article I
   c. Article II, Section 2
   d. Article III, Section 1

2. Congress established the federal district courts and the federal circuit courts of appeals when the legislators enacted the _____.
   a. Civil Rights bill
   b. Judiciary Act of 1789
   c. Courts Law
   d. Articles of Confederation

3. The federal district courts have jurisdiction over cases involving the following federal crimes:
   a. Bank robbery
   b. Illegal interstate commerce
   c. Counterfeiting
   d. All of the above

4. The United States is divided geographically into _____ federal judicial circuits.
   a. 11
   b. 10
   c. 12
   d. 15

5. Each circuit court normally hears cases in panels of _____ judges.
    a. 3
    b. 1
    c. 5
    d. 8

Projects You Can Do

Use the Internet or your local public library to learn:

1. Which federal district court serves the city in which you live and which federal circuit court(s) serve your state? Where are these courts located?
2. What types of cases has your federal circuit court recently handled?
3. About a judge who was recently appointed to one of these courts. What was that person's previous job, before being appointed a judge?

The Supreme Court

The Supreme Court heads the judicial branch, and it is the final authority for interpreting the Constitution. All federal courts and state supreme courts must follow the Supreme Court's interpretation of federal laws and the Constitution. The Supreme Court also has the power to review congressional, presidential, and state legislation actions to ensure that they follow the guidelines of the Constitution. The Supreme Court, however, does not have the authority to:

- interpret state law
- decide issues arising under state constitutions
- supervise state court operations.

> The republic endures and this is a symbol of its faith.
>
> —Inscription on the Supreme Court Building

As we have seen, the Constitution provides for a strong national government, but at the same time, that strong government must guarantee its citizens certain freedoms and rights. Because the Constitution is a framework rather than a complete set of detailed laws, it often needs to be interpreted by the judicial branch when the competing interests of a strong government and citizens' freedoms desire different laws.

Surf's up...

Check out the following sites to learn more about the Supreme Court:

bensguide.gpo.gov/6-8/government/national/scourt.html

uscourts.gov/supremecourt.html

Because of this balance, the Supreme Court's most important responsibility is *judicial review*. The Court has been given the power to review court cases, as well as legislative and executive branch actions that raise *constitutional questions*, which are legal issues that require an interpretation of the Constitution to decide them. Judicial review gives the Supreme Court the ultimate authority to decide some of the most important problems that have faced our country.

Article III, Section 1, gives the Supreme Court authority over the lower federal courts. Similarly, the Supremacy Clause of Article VI grants the Court the power of judicial review over the states:

> This Constitution, and the Laws of the United States which shall be made in Pursuance thereof: and all Treaties made, or which shall be made, under the Authority of the United States, shall be the supreme Law of the Land; and the Judges in every State shall be bound thereby, any Thing in the Constitution or Laws of any State to the Contrary notwithstanding.

By contrast, the Constitution doesn't specifically grant the Court the power of judicial review over the actions of Congress and the president. So, where does it get the power to review and, if necessary, declare actions of these branches unconstitutional? The answer is from the Court's own interpretation of the Constitution. In 1803, Chief Justice John Marshall wrote in the Court's decision in *Marbury v. Madison* that the Constitution's writers intended for the Constitution to be the supreme law of the nation; therefore, no one, including even the Congress or the president, should be allowed to violate the Constitution. Any legislation or government action that is contrary to the guidelines of the Constitution is said to be unconstitutional. Because the Court had the power to interpret the Constitution, it also must have the power to judge legislative and executive actions. As a result, this was the first time the Court declared a law illegal (part of the Judiciary Act of 1789). Since then, we have accepted that judicial review includes not only the power to review the decisions of lower courts but also the power to declare actions of the legislative and executive branches unconstitutional.

Things to Think About

1. Do you think that it's a good idea for the Supreme Court to have the power to declare decisions by state supreme courts illegal if the Court thinks they are unconstitutional? Or should this right belong only to the state?
2. Do you think that the writers of the Constitution meant to give the Supreme Court and the judicial branch the power to review the actions of Congress or a president? If they did, why didn't they specifically mention this power?
3. What things do you think the justices consider when they try to determine if an action of Congress is unconstitutional?

The Supreme Court justices

When vacancies arise in the various courts, presidents have the constitutional power to appoint all federal judges, including the nine *Supreme Court justices*. Like all federal judges, the Supreme Court justices serve for a life term. Although the Constitution doesn't specify qualifications for Supreme Court justices, from the beginning, the justices have all been lawyers, and most have practiced law or served in government before serving on the Supreme Court. Because Supreme Court justices serve for life and their decisions have a major impact on American society, their appointments are probably the most important that a president makes. Typically, the justices have belonged to the same political party as the president who appointed them. Even more important than the nominee's political party, however, is that person's *judicial philosophy*—that is, whether a nominee believes the Supreme Court should be active in its judicial review, or allow the states and the other branches of government to have more of a final say in their decisions. The philosophy also includes the nominee's stand on the issues that might come before the Court. For example, in the recent past, the Court has decided many important issues, such as anti-segregation, school prayer, and freedom of speech. The president must also consider whether a majority of the Senate will approve the nominee during the confirmation process. The attention given the Supreme Court nominee's confirmation process in the Senate reflects how important the Court's decisions are.

Also, when there's a vacancy, the president appoints one justice as Chief Justice of the Supreme Court. The *Chief Justice* is in charge of the Court. The other eight justices are *associate justices*.

Did You Know?

William Taft served as Chief Justice after serving as president.

A Minute with Senator WordSmart
Set # 3

Take a minute and review the meanings of some new words by matching the word with its definition.

1. Supreme Court

2. Judicial branch

3. Constitutional questions

4. Federal district courts

5. Federal circuit courts of appeals

6. Circuit

a. Contrary to the guidelines of the Constitution.

b. Legal issues that require an interpretation of the Constitution.

c. System of courts that consists of district courts, circuit courts of appeals, and the Supreme Court.

d. Court of highest authority in our country.

e. The appeals courts for the federal district courts.

f. Geographic area under the jurisdiction of a federal court of appeals.

7. Unconstitutional

    g. Trial courts that hear cases involving federal law, as well as appeals from state supreme courts.

8. Supreme Court justices

    h. The justice in charge of the Supreme Court.

9. Judicial review

    i. Judges who sit on the Supreme Court.

10. Judicial philosophy

    j. The power of the Supreme Court to review lower court cases, as well as declare certain actions of the legislative and executive branches unconstitutional.

11. Chief justice

    k. How a Supreme Court justice views the role of the Court regarding the power of judicial review.

The early Supreme Court

George Washington appointed John Jay of New York as the Supreme Court's first Chief Justice. Originally, there was one Chief Justice and five associate justices. Subsequently, the

JOHN JAY   GEORGE WASHINGTON

number of justices changed six times before settling at the present nine in 1869. Besides John Jay, Washington appointed the following people to the first Supreme Court.

Supreme Court Justice	Home State
John Jay (Chief Justice)	New York
John Rutledge	South Carolina
William Cushing	Massachusetts
John Blair	Virginia
James Iredell	North Carolina
James Wilson	Pennsylvania

Did You Know?

In its entire history, the Supreme Court has only had 16 Chief Justices.

The Supreme Court first met on February 1, 1790, in the Merchants Exchange Building in New York City, which was our nation's capital before Washington, D.C. The Court spent its first year organizing itself and the rest of the judiciary branch. The first cases reached the Court the following year, and the justices handed down their first *judicial opinion* or ruling in 1792.

Once the Capitol was constructed in Washington, D.C., the justices and their staffs met in various rooms of the Capitol and elsewhere to hear cases and conduct their work. In 1935, the Court moved into its own building, which had been built across the street from the Capitol.

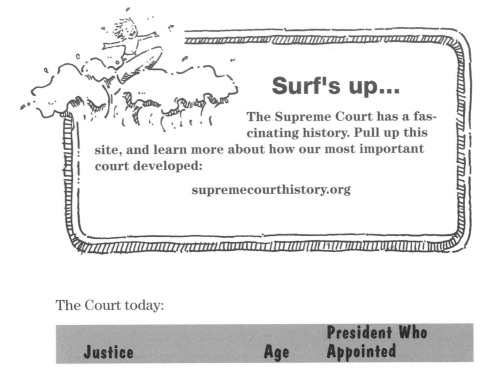

Surf's up...

The Supreme Court has a fascinating history. Pull up this site, and learn more about how our most important court developed:

supremecourthistory.org

The Court today:

Justice	Age	President Who Appointed
William Rehnquist (Chief Justice)	79	Richard Nixon
John Stevens	83	Gerald Ford
Sandra Day O'Connor	73	Ronald Reagan
Antonin Scalia	67	Ronald Reagan
Anthony Kennedy	67	Ronald Reagan
David Souter	64	George H. W. Bush
Clarence Thomas	55	George H. W. Bush
Ruth Bader Ginsburg	70	Bill Clinton
Steven Breyer	65	Bill Clinton

The Choice Is Yours
Set # 4

To check your understanding of the previous material, answer the following questions by selecting the letter of the correct answer.

1. The Supreme Court has the authority to determine which of the following are unconstitutional?
   a. A federal law enacted by Congress
   b. The decision of a state supreme court
   c. An action of the president
   d. All of the above

2. To evaluate a Supreme Court nominee properly, the president and the Senate should most consider the _____ of the nominee.
   a. height
   b. judicial philosophy
   c. school grades
   d. birthplace

3. There are _____ justices on the Supreme Court.
   a. 3
   b. 12
   c. 9
   d. 8

4. The first Chief Justice of the Supreme Court was _____.
   a. George Washington
   b. Thomas Jefferson
   c. John Jay
   d. John Adams

5. How many of the justices on the current Supreme Court are women?
   a. 2
   b. 0
   c. 1
   d. 3

Did You Know?

In 1954, the Court banned racial segregation (forcing people to be apart because of their race) in public schools with its judicial opinion in *Brown v. Board of Education of Topeka*. The ruling started a long process of desegregating schools and many other areas of American society.

Selection of cases for the Supreme Court

Typically, lawyers appeal lower court cases to the Supreme Court through a writ of certiorari. A ***writ of certiorari*** is a request for review of the case based on important constitutional and legal issues raised by the court's decision. The lawyers who communicate with the Court in these writs try to convince the justices that the case's decision violates federal law or the Constitution. The justices discuss the writs in conferences held twice a week. Under the ***rule of four***, only four of the nine justices have to agree to put the case on the docket. The ***docket*** is the Supreme Court's schedule of cases to review.

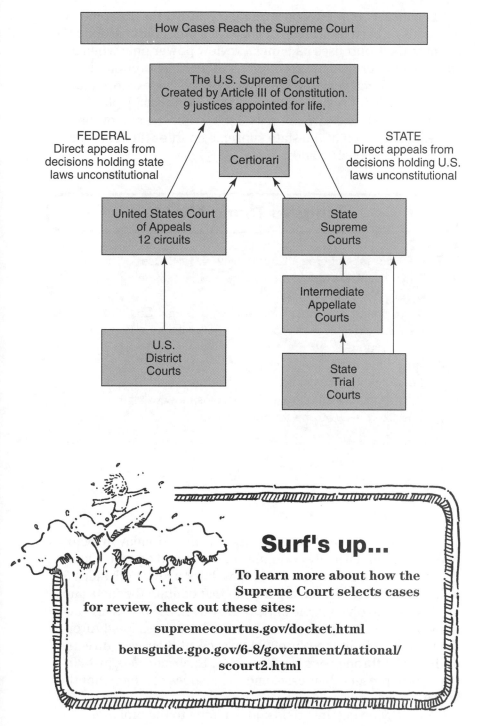

How Cases Reach the Supreme Court

The U.S. Supreme Court
Created by Article III of Constitution.
9 justices appointed for life.

FEDERAL
Direct appeals from
decisions holding state
laws unconstitutional

Certiorari

STATE
Direct appeals from
decisions holding U.S.
laws unconstitutional

United States Court
of Appeals
12 circuits

State
Supreme
Courts

U.S.
District
Courts

Intermediate
Appellate
Courts

State
Trial
Courts

Surf's up...

**To learn more about how the
Supreme Court selects cases
for review, check out these sites:**

supremecourtus.gov/docket.html

**bensguide.gpo.gov/6-8/government/national/
scourt2.html**

189

Because a Supreme Court ruling can affect the outcome of hundreds or even thousands of cases in lower courts around the country, the Court uses its judicial review power only when a case involves critical interpretations of the Constitution or federal law. Each year, the Supreme Court receives more than 7,000 requests for review; however, the Court usually places fewer than 100 cases a year on its docket. For the rest of the cases, the decision of the state supreme court or the federal circuit court of appeals stands.

Things to Think About

1. Why does the Supreme Court review so few cases each year?
2. Do you think the rule of four is a good idea? Should the number be fewer or more?
3. Do you think it's a good idea that the Supreme Court justices are appointed for life? Would it be better if they served for a 10-year term?
4. Should the voters elect them?
5. If a justice's judicial philosophy is to rarely interfere with the federal government's legislative process, how will this justice most likely view most writs of certiorari?

In Court

The term of the Court begins, by law, the first Monday in October of each year and usually continues until the end of June. Once the Court schedules a case for review, lawyers for both sides file *briefs*, which are written arguments that contain the facts and legal issues involved in the appeal. However, the briefs are anything but brief. Many have been hundreds of pages long! After the lawyers submit their briefs, they present their case directly to the Court through *oral arguments*. Each side gets just 30 minutes to present their case, and the justices can interrupt the lawyers to ask questions.

After reviewing the briefs and listening to the oral arguments, the justices discuss the case. Because it is so important for our judicial process to be consistent, the justices' decisions build on principles established from previous court rulings. We refer to this process as *precedent*.

Once the discussions are over, the justices vote. The court's decision is referred to as the *majority opinion* because it is the decision on which a majority of judges agreed, meaning five out of nine justices in a full Court. At this point, the justices begin writing the majority opinion and a dissenting opinion (if there is one). The *dissenting opinion* is the opinion of the minority of judges. Both opinions state the judges' decision and their reasons. However, only the majority opinion becomes the final authority.

A Minute with Senator WordSmart
Set # 4

Take a minute and review the meanings of some new words by matching the word with its definition.

1. Writ of Certiorari
      a. A request for the review of a case based on important constitutional and legal issues raised by the lower court's decision.

2. Rule of four
      b. Deciding a case based on principles established in previous cases.

3. Docket
      c. Only four of nine Supreme Court justices have to agree to hear a case before it is placed on the docket.

4. Briefs
      d. Written arguments submitted to the Supreme Court that contain facts and legal issues.

5. Oral arguments

6. Precedent

7. Majority opinion

8. Dissenting opinion

e. The decision agreed upon by a minority of the Supreme Court justices.

f. The Court's schedule of cases to review.

g. Thirty-minute presentations made by attorneys to the Supreme Court justices.

h. The decision agreed upon by a majority of the justices, making it the ruling of the Supreme Court.

Enforcement of the decision

The Supreme Court has no power to enforce its decisions. The Court can't call out the army or force Congress or the president to obey; rather, the Court relies on the executive and legislative branches to carry out its rulings. However, our system of government works, because both of the other branches and the state governments follow the judicial branch's rulings. We are a nation ruled by laws.

Projects You Can Do

Use your local public library or the Internet to:

1. Learn more about the facts and the decisions in one or more of these following cases:

   - *Cherokee Nation v. Georgia* (1831). (The Cherokee lands are a domestic nation within the boundaries of the United States.)
   - *Schneck v. U.S.* (1919). (There are no absolute freedoms; all freedoms must be judged according to the circumstances.)
   - *Brown v. Board of Education of Topeka* (1954). (Public schools must not be segregated.)

- *Gideon v. Wainright* (1963). (The government must provide anyone charged with a felony (serious crime) a lawyer if the accused can't afford one.)
- *Miranda v. Arizona* (1966). (Accused individuals have the right to remain silent and must be informed of their rights.)

2. Learn about the judicial philosophies of the justices now sitting on the Supreme Court.
3. What were the issues involved in some recently decided Supreme Court cases?

We have learned about the Constitution and the three branches of government that it created. Now, let's learn how we elect our representatives.

CHAPTER SEVEN

Elections and Political Parties

VOTE

DEMOCRATS

REPUBLICANS

VALUE OF ELECTIONS

An *election* is a regularly scheduled process that allows citizens to select people to represent them within the local, state, and national government. The administrative system surrounding and supporting elections is referred to as the *electoral system*.

Why hold elections? Why not just have everyone participate in the government? The answer is that our country has too many people for each person to have a direct role in government, meaning we can't have a *direct democracy*. Instead, we have a repre-  sentative democracy. In a *representative democracy*, the people select their represen- tatives, and the representatives make the laws and run the government. (Refer to Chapter One for more discussion on direct and representative democracies.) Because we have a representative democracy, we need a good way to select our representa- tives as well as a good way to find qualified representatives.

At election time, each *candidate*, the person wishing to represent the people from a specific area, aims to convince the voters that he or she will make a better representative. Elections encourage elected repre- sentatives to do a good job and communicate with their *constituents*—that is, the citizens whom they are representing. If they don't represent their constituents well, they won't be elected again. Citizens express themselves through their *vote*.

A Minute with Senator WordSmart
Set # 1

Take a minute to make sure that you understand the meanings of the new words. Match the word in the left-hand column with its definition in the right-hand column by drawing a line from the word to its definition. If you want to check your work, review the Answer Key in the back of the book.

1. Election

2. Electoral system

3. Direct democracy

4. Representative democracy

5. Candidate

6. Constituents

7. Vote

a. The citizens whom a government representative represents.

b. The administrative system surrounding and supporting elections.

c. Each person has a say in the government.

d. An individual wishing to be a representative of the people from his or her area.

e. A system of government in which the people select representatives who will make the laws and run the government.

f. To select a candidate in an election.

g. A regularly scheduled process in which citizens select their local, state, and national government representatives.

THE ELECTORAL SYSTEM

In the United States, we hold elections at regular intervals because we want the representative selection process to be predictable. We need to know when, where, and how we can tell our representatives what kind of job we think they're doing. If elections were held infrequently or irregularly, people wouldn't use them to communicate their feelings about their representatives. They might resort to more disruptive means, possibly even violence.

The Constitution has set the term of office for the U.S. House of Representatives at two years, the Senate at six years, and the presidency at four years. Article I, Section 4 then leaves it up to individual states to cooperate and determine the timing, location, and the rules of the elections. As a result—and for convenience—we elect our state and local representatives at the same time as the national elections, which is the Tuesday after the first Monday in November. That Tuesday in November is Election Day across the United States.

Why is Election Day held in November? For much of our history, most Americans were farmers. Election organizers decided that November would be the most convenient month for farmers to travel to the *polls*, the places designated by the state where their citizens would cast their votes. By November, the fall harvest was over, but in most of the nation, the weather was still mild enough to permit travel over country roads.

Why is Election Day on a Tuesday? Because most farmers had to travel a long way on those country roads to the polls, many would have to start out the day before the voting. If Monday were Election Day, many people would have had to begin travel on Sunday, which would have interfered with their church services. Therefore, they selected the next day, Tuesday.

Surf's up...

If you want to learn more about our electoral system, glide into this site:

fec.gov/pages/faqs.htm

learning.loc.gov/learn/features/election/home.html

State laws list the qualifications of candidates and the way the elections should be run, including registration procedures, the location of polls, and even the way the *ballots* (the cards on which the voters select the candidates) must look. State and local governments, usually through *election boards*, organize and run elections. These boards, which consist of people appointed by their state legislatures, staff the polls, check the eligibility of voters, and count the votes after the election is over. States also determine the boundaries for their *congressional districts*, which are areas within the state that contain nearly the same number of people. (Refer to Chapter Four for more discussion on congressional districts.) Some states also provide for referendum voting. The *referendum* is a process that allows citizens to vote on proposed laws or other governmental actions, such as limiting state and local tax rates, or proposed social services for certain groups. Referendums permit voters, rather than state legislatures, to make certain laws. The referendum is one of our few examples of direct democracy.

Did You Know?

In 1898, South Dakota became the first state to allow referendums.

Things to Think About

1. What if we voted from home on the computer or mailed in our ballot, rather than traveled to the polls? What would be the advantages and disadvantages?

2. Think of other ways to select representatives. How are these ways similar and different from elections?

Participating in elections

The right to vote, or **suffrage**, is an important right because it allows people to participate in elections, and therefore, in our representative government. Today, U.S. citizens older than age 18, with the exception of convicted criminals, have the right to vote. During the early years of our nation, state laws permitted only white men older than age 21 to vote. Also, many states allowed only those men who owned property or paid an annual tax, called a poll tax, to vote. By the end of the Civil War, however, these restrictions began to disappear, at least as they affected voting by white men. During the time of the Civil War, African-Americans were given the right to vote in most Northern states. After the Civil War, the Fifteenth Amendment, ratified in 1870, secured the right for African-Americans throughout the nation to vote.

Despite the Fifteenth Amendment, the states of the former Confederacy kept African-Americans from voting through an illegal, but unfortunately effective, system of discrimination, which used various tactics, such as poll taxes, reading tests, and property qualifications. This system persisted virtually unopposed until the 1950s and 1960s when the Civil Rights Movement pressed for full voting rights for African-Americans. The movement's efforts achieved success with the enactment of the 1965 Voting Rights Act, which provided for the U.S. Department of Justice to oversee registration of voters and election in states with histories of discrimination against African-Americans and other minority citizens.

Women achieved the right to vote in 1920, through the passage of the Nineteenth Amendment. Women, too, were forced to work hard and confront groups opposed to change to earn their right to vote. The most recent achievement in voting rights belongs to young people. In 1971, the Twenty-Sixth Amendment lowered the voting age from 21 to 18.

The Choice Is Yours
Set # 1

To check your understanding of the previous material, answer the following questions by selecting the letter of the correct answer. If you want to check your work, refer to the Answer Key in the back of the book.

1. The _____ Amendment gave African-Americans the right to vote.
   a. Nineteenth
   b. Fifteenth
   c. Thirteenth
   d. Twenty-Sixth

2. During the early years of our country, only _____ were allowed to vote.
   a. adults older than age 18
   b. certain white men older than age 21
   c. men
   d. white men and women

3. Women achieved the right to vote with the passage of the _____ Amendment.
   a. Twenty-Sixth
   b. Fifteenth
   c. Thirteenth
   d. Nineteenth

4. The _____ Amendment lowered the voting age from 21 years old to 18 years old.
   a. Tenth
   b. Thirteenth
   c. Fifteenth
   d. Twenty-Sixth

5. Election Day is on _____.
   a. the first day in April
   b. the Tuesday after the first Monday in November
   c. the day after Thanksgiving
   d. September 15

Counting the votes

For most elections, the winner doesn't necessarily need to have a *majority of votes* (more than half the votes cast). Our country has a *plurality electoral system*. In an election where there are more than two candidates, the winner may have only a *plurality of votes* (the larger number of votes).

A Minute with Senator WordSmart
Set # 2

Take a minute to make sure that you understand the meanings of the new words. Match the word in the left-hand column with its definition in the right-hand column.

1. Polls

2. Ballots
3. Congressional district

a. The cards on which the voters select the candidates.
b. The larger number of votes.
c. The people appointed by their state legislatures to organize and run elections in the state.

4. Election board

    d. A process that allows citizens to vote on proposed laws or other governmental actions, thereby empowering citizens to make the laws, rather than leaving it to state legislatures.

5. Referendum

    e. More than half of the votes cast.

6. Suffrage

    f. The places designated by the state where its citizens must cast their votes.

7. Majority of votes

    g. Areas in the state that contain nearly the same number of people.

8. Plurality of votes

    h. Electoral system where the winning candidate only needs to receive more votes than any other candidate.

9. Plurality electoral system

    i. The right to vote.

Projects You Can Do

1. Select a country and learn how they elect their government leaders. How do the leaders represent their citizens?
2. Many states have referendum voting. Learn about some recent referendums. What were the issues? How did the voters respond? Why did the states choose to put the issue up for referendum and not through the legislative process?
3. Learn about the suffrage movements of

   - African-Americans
   - Women.

   How were these movements similar? Who opposed them and why?

POLITICAL PARTIES AND THE ELECTORAL SYSTEM

Political parties are organizations that seek to accomplish specific goals within the government by electing its members to office. Once elected, those representatives try to achieve the goals of their party through legislation and government programs. Because we determine election winners by the number of votes they receive, political parties want as many people (voters) as possible, so the parties are made up of citizens who differ in race, religion, age, and economic and social background, but who have the same goals for their government and their country.

Political parties have become essential to our electoral system because they:

- recruit and encourage people to run for office
- organize primary elections so party members can select their candidates for general election
- support their candidates who reach general election
- write *platforms*, which state their goals and their positions on key issues.

As a result, political parties have played a crucial role in educating Americans about issues and in encouraging people to vote.

Surf's up...

Check out the platforms of the Republican and Democrat parties at these sites:

Republican Platform
mc.org/GOPInfo/Platform/2000platform.htm

Democrat Platform
democrats.org/about/platform.html

Most members participate in the election process only by voting for their party's candidates. However, some members become more active and work as officials in the party or volunteer to persuade people to vote for the party's candidates. The most ambitious members decide to run for office.

For most of our history, we've had a competitive *two-party system*, which means that two major political parties were the most influential and provided the candidates that became representatives. *Third*, *or independent*, *parties*, political parties

other than the two major parties, continue to exist, but have never been influential. Because independent party candidates rarely win an election, people who vote for them do so more to make a statement than trying to elect a candidate.

Oddly enough, the founders of our country opposed political parties. They viewed parties as "factions" or groups that would try to manipulate the voters and government for their own selfish ends. The founders wanted people with different individual philosophies to take part in the government, rather than people who were members of a group. For example, George Washington included in his cabinet men who disagreed with him about the goals of the country. Nevertheless, by the early nineteenth century, political parties had become powerful. Their accomplishments included:

- organizing members of Congress so that party members all voted the same on proposed laws
- convincing people to go the polls and vote
- strengthening the presidency beyond the point which the writers of the Constitution had imagined by creating an alliance between the parties in the executive and legislative branches

Things to Think About

1. Learn about some independent or third parties. Were they successful? Why did they form?

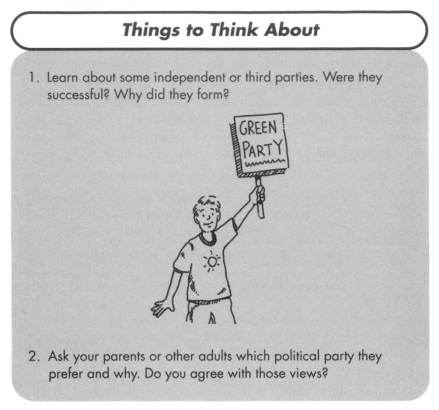

2. Ask your parents or other adults which political party they prefer and why. Do you agree with those views?

POLITICAL PARTY HISTORY

Thomas Jefferson and James Madison began the Republican Party, which favored a limited national government. Opposing this view were the members of the Federalist Party, such as Alexander Hamilton and John Adams, who favored a strong and active national government. The Federalist Party gradually lost power. After the War of 1812, the Republican Party (which had become known as the Democratic-Republican Party) remained as the only national political party. Before long, however, the two-party system reemerged as Democratic-Republicans started disagreeing on several issues, including economic policy. The followers of Henry Clay and John Quincy Adams, who supported large industry and wanted the national government to get involved in the country's economy, were called National Republicans. Their opponents, who eventually united behind the presidential candidacy of Andrew Jackson, came to be known as the Democratic Party. The Democrats originally favored small businesses and farmers. (The Democratic Party actually traces its roots and philosophy to the Jefferson Republican Party—it's kind of confusing, but that's politics!) Since the mid-1850s, the two major parties in the United States have been the Republican and Democratic parties.

The structure of our government encouraged the formation of political parties. The system of checks and balances established by the Constitution made executive and legislative cooperation necessary; otherwise, each branch would keep the other from accomplishing anything. Further, our federal system, which divides legislative powers between the national and state governments, also made it necessary for representatives in the national and state governments to work together.

The Choice Is Yours
Set # 2

To check your understanding of the previous material, answer the following questions by selecting the letter of the correct answer.

1. All national elections in the United States use the _____ system.
   a. plurality vote
   b. majority vote
   c. electoral college
   d. "picking names out of a hat"

2. The table below shows the votes received by three candidates in a national election. Who won?

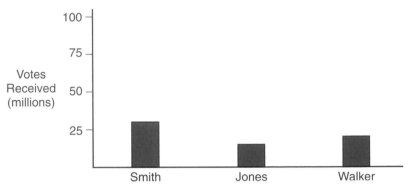

a. Smith
b. Jones
c. Walker
d. There is no winner because no candidate received the majority of votes.

3. There are _____ major political parties in the United States.
a. three
b. two
c. four
d. several

4. The modern Democratic Party's first presidential candidate was _____.
a. George Washington
b. Bill Clinton
c. Andrew Jackson
d. James Madison

5. Alexander Hamilton and John Adams were _____.
a. Democrats
b. Republicans
c. Communists
d. Federalists

Projects You Can Do

1. Talk to someone who works for one of the political parties. What do they do? Why do they feel their work is important?
2. Learn about the similarities and differences between the Republican Party and Democrat Party.
3. Use the Internet or your local public library to learn more about the histories of the Democrat and Republican parties.

POLITICAL PARTIES AND VOTER PARTICIPATION

Compared with citizens in other democracies, voter participation in elections in the United States is low. Slightly more than 50 percent of our eligible voters participate in presidential elections. Worse yet, barely 25 percent of eligible voters vote in congressional elections during nonpresidential election years. By contrast, in European nations, voter turnout consistently exceeds 80 percent.

Things to Think About

1. How do you think this county's low voter participation affects the way our representatives communicate with us?
2. What do you think are the reasons for the low voter participation rate in the United States? Do these reasons exist in Europe?
3. Why is a low voter participation rate bad for our representative democracy?

It wasn't always like this in the United States. During the nineteenth century, ***political party machines***, which were hundreds of thousands of workers employed by the major political parties, organized and brought voters to the polls so that they would vote for the machine's candidates. The machines were very successful, and in some areas, voter turnout approached 90 percent.

The
New
Political
Machine

Despite their success, political party machines became too costly for the political parties to maintain. Political machines began to decline in strength in the early twentieth century and have largely disappeared today. Without the thousands of party workers to encourage voters to go to the polls—and even take them there if necessary—many people don't vote. Furthermore, as the political party machines declined, so did the political parties to a degree. Today, parties are less important. Slightly more than one-third of all Americans don't feel as if they belong to, or identify with, one of the major parties. As loyalty to political parties declines, voter participation is also likely to decline.

A Minute with Senator WordSmart

Set # 3

Take a minute to make sure that you understand the meanings of the new words. Match the word in the left-hand column with its definition in the right-hand column. If you want to check your work, review the Answer Key in the back of the book.

1. Political party

2. Platform

3. Two-party system

4. Third, or independent, parties

5. Political party machine

a. Hundreds of thousands of workers employed by the major political parties.

b. Parties that are not one of the two major parties.

c. This states the goals of the political party and its position on key issues.

d. Organizations that have specific goals and seek to accomplish these goals within the government by electing members to office.

e. Two major political parties that are the most influential and provide the candidates who become representatives.

Surf's up...

Check out this site to learn more about how political parties interact with voters:

learning.loc.gov/learn/features/election/voters.html

PURSUIT OF OFFICE

Incumbents (those individuals who are currently serving as representatives in government offices) are rarely challenged for *nomination*, which is the right to represent their party in the general election. On the other hand, those candidates from the other party, the *challengers*, must compete with candidates from their own party in *primary elections* so that they represent their party against the incumbent in the general election. The United States is one of the few nations that hold primary elections before the general election campaign. Most democratic nations elect their political leaders in general elections. The primary election is like a qualifying election for the general election. It is in the *general election* that the voters select from the candidates who won their primary elections. They decide which one will represent them in a particular government office. Both the incumbents and challengers must campaign in the months before the general election.

A *campaign* is an organized attempt by the candidate to gain support to be elected. Campaigns are expensive, costing hundreds of thousands of dollars, and sometimes millions of dollars. Developing a campaign requires asking friends and acquaintances, as well as special interest groups and your political party for money.

Once the candidate is confident that the necessary money can be raised, the next step is to bring people into the campaign and create a *campaign organization*. These are the people who work to get the candidate elected. The most important person in the candidate's organization is the *campaign manager*. The campaign manager develops the strategy for the campaign. The campaign manager develops and applies this campaign strategy by, among other things:

- conducting surveys to learn what the voters like and dislike
- buying television time and other advertising to help make the voters aware of the candidate's views and qualifications
- arranging for the candidate to meet with various interest groups and groups of voters.

The goal of the strategy is to get the candidate elected by making the voters aware of the candidate's views and characteristics that appeal to a large percentage of voters.

A Minute with Senator WordSmart
Set # 4

Take a minute to make sure that you understand the meanings of the new words. Match the word in the left-hand column with its definition in the right-hand column.

1. Incumbent

2. Nomination

3. Challenger

a. The selection by a candidate's political party members to represent the party in the general election.

b. A candidate who isn't an incumbent.

c. An individual who is currently serving in a political office.

4. Primary elections

   d. The organized attempt by the candidate to gain support to be elected.

5. General election

   e. The person who develops the strategy for a candidate's campaign.

6. Campaign

   f. The people who work together to get the candidate elected.

7. Campaign organization

   g. An election where the voters choose between candidates from different parties. The winner will be their representative in the particular government office.

8. Campaign manager

   h. An election where the voters from each political party select their candidate who will run in the general election.

CONGRESSIONAL ELECTIONS

Not every elected official in the House of Representative and Senate must campaign at the same time. Every member of the House of Representatives must run for election every two years; however, because senators are elected for a six-year term, only one-third of the senators are involved in the election. This makes it easier on the voters and the entire electoral system. None-theless, because 435 seats in the House of Representatives and 15 to 20 seats in the Senate are up for election, more than 900 candidates, both incumbents and challengers, will be competing in congressional elections throughout the country.

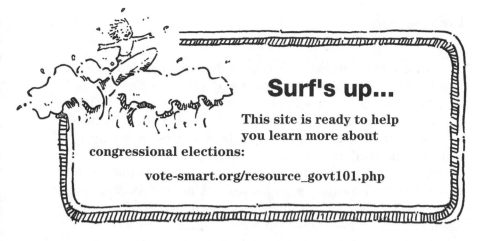

Surf's up...

This site is ready to help you learn more about congressional elections:

vote-smart.org/resource_govt101.php

The House of Representatives

Most House of Representatives incumbents win reelection. Why is keeping a House seat so much easier than gaining it? The answer is incumbents have several advantages that help them get reelected, which include:

- free mailings to constituents (called the *franking privilege*)
- the free use of broadcast studios to record television and radio ads
- a large staff that keeps in contact with the constituents in the congressional district.

Because incumbents win so often, we gain a significant number of our new House representatives when incumbents die, decide to retire, or seek some other office. One other way of gaining new representatives is through *redistricting*, which is the redrawing of congressional district boundary lines based on changes in population. This redrawing occurs once every 10 years when new census data is available. Redistricting promotes change in that it increases the possibility that incumbents will be forced to run in campaigns in districts that have different boundaries and, thus, different voters who may not like the incumbent. Also, if the state's population increases significantly, new districts may be formed, requiring representatives.

The Senate

By contrast, competition for a seat in the Senate is much more intense. The 6-year term, the power and influence that comes from being 1 lawmaker out of only 100, rather than 1 out of 435, and the national exposure make a Senate seat more valuable. Therefore, challengers and their political parties are willing to expend a lot of effort and money campaigning.

Incumbency is still an advantage for senators, although not as much as for House representatives. Incumbent senators have the same campaigning advantages as the incumbent House representatives that were listed earlier. However, these may not help much when confronting a well-funded campaign by a challenger.

Things to Think About

1. In Congress, on the whole, many incumbents win, causing some critics to say that we have a "permanent Congress." One solution is to limit the number of terms a legislator may serve. Is this a good idea? On the other hand, is it bad that many incumbents win?

2. Refer to Chapter Four's discussion of representatives and senators. A senator serves a more diverse constituency. How might this make a senatorial campaign different from a representative's campaign?

> ## Projects You Can Do

1. Learn about the recent elections of your state's two senators. Were the elections close? What were the issues?
2. Learn about a challenger who defeated an incumbent for a congressional seat. What strategy did the challenger use to succeed?
3. Imagine that you are a campaign manager for a Senate candidate. How would you go about running your candidate's campaign?

PURSUIT OF THE PRESIDENCY

Running for the office of president requires many of the same ingredients that running a successful election to Congress does: a lot of money to run a campaign, good campaign organization, a good campaign manager, and the ability to become recognized in a positive way by many voters. Just like with a congressional election, a presidential candidate must be nominated, however, because the presidency is a nationwide election; the nomination process takes longer and requires more difficult and expensive campaigning.

Winning the party's presidential nomination

Candidates and their campaign managers must develop a strategy to win delegates from the numerous presidential primaries and caucuses. Candidates win their party's nomination through successful showings in presidential primaries and state caucuses.

To select candidates from each party for the general election, more than three-fourths of the states use a presidential primary. A *presidential primary* is a statewide election in which voters from each party select the candidate whom they would like to see represent their party in the general election. The candidate with the most votes is awarded the state's delegates. These delegates then vote for the candidate at the party's national convention. The candidate with the most delegates wins the nomination—and, thus, the right to run in the national presidential election. The rest of the states use caucuses to help them with their nomination decision. A *state caucus* is a statewide meeting of party members and supporters of various candidates. A state caucus differs from a primary. Rather than have a statewide election, a small group of party officials select the candidate. Regardless of whether a state uses a primary or a caucus to select its candidate, the candidate selected receives the votes of the state's delegates at the party's national convention.

The national party convention

The next step to the presidency is the national party convention. A *national party convention* is the national meeting of the delegates pledged to the candidates as the result of victories in state primaries and caucuses. Each party holds its convention in the summer before the presidential election to nominate its presidential and vice presidential candidates.

National party conventions follow standard rules and routines. On the first day, party leaders deliver speeches promoting the party's platform and candidates and criticizing the opposition's. The second day is spent reviewing the convention's procedural rules and the party's platform. On the third day, the presidential candidate is nominated. Everyone at the convention already knows who it will be because the candidate who has earned most delegates as a result of victories in the primaries and caucuses is designated the party's presidential nominee. The convention ends on the fourth day with the presidential nominee selecting a running mate who will serve as vice president if the nominee is elected. Together, the presidential nominee and the vice presidential nominee are known as a *ticket*. In the past, the presidential nominee chose a running mate who would "balance the ticket"; that is, appeal to a different set of voters than the presidential nominee. For instance, a presidential nominee who is from the North may select a running mate who is from the South. Lately, however, vice presidential running mates have been selected on their ability to step into the role of the presidency, if necessary. (Refer to Chapter Five for a discussion of the vice presidents who had to take over the presidency.) Finally, the convention ends with the presidential candidate's acceptance speech.

A Minute with Senator WordSmart
Set # 5

Take a minute to make sure that you understand the meanings of the new words. Match the word in the left-hand column with its definition in the right-hand column.

1. Franking privilege

2. Redistricting

3. Presidential primary

4. State caucus

5. National party convention

a. Redrawing of boundary lines for congressional districts based on changes in population.

b. A statewide election in which voters from each party select the candidate whom they would like to see represent their party in the general election. The candidate with the most votes is awarded the state's delegates.

c. A statewide meeting of party officials in which they select whom they would like to be their party's candidate in the national presidential election.

d. The free use of the mail for official Congressional business.

e. A party's presidential and vice presidential nominees.

6. Ticket

f. The national meeting of the delegates pledged to the candidates as the result of victories in state primaries and caucuses. Each party's convention occurs in the summer before the presidential election to nominate its presidential and vice presidential candidates.

Things to Think About

1. Once the primaries and state caucuses are concluded, the candidates know how many delegates are pledged to them, and whether they've won their party's nomination. Why do parties continue to have conventions if their party's presidential candidate is already known?
2. What are the advantages and disadvantages of the presidential candidate selecting a running mate, rather than the political party's voters?

The presidential election

The final step is for the nominated presidential candidate and vice presidential candidate to run against the other party's ticket in a general election. The general election is loaded with a great deal of campaigning, many television ads, and a few public televised debates. The *presidential debates* are a series of meetings where the candidates confront one another, and the voters can watch and listen to them discuss various issues. These debates provide opportunities for the public to determine each candidate's qualifications.

Electing the winning ticket

We elect our president and vice president through the electoral college. The *electoral college* is a group of persons called *electors*, *or delegates*, and each represents an *electoral vote*. The electors are selected by their states to officially elect the president and vice president. The number of electoral votes in each state is equal to its number of representatives in both houses of Congress. The writers of the Constitution devised this system to remove the choice of president from the direct vote of the people.

Did You Know?

Candidates who win a plurality (the most votes) of the popular vote in a state win all that state's electoral votes, except in Nebraska and Maine, which award electoral votes to the winner in each congressional district, plus two electoral votes for whoever earns the most votes in the state as a whole.

Under the electoral college system, a candidate could receive the most individual votes (the popular vote), and yet not have enough electoral votes to win the election. The system was designed to prevent a candidate who is immensely popular in a particular region of the country from winning the election based on personal success in that region. We want a candidate who represents more than one region of the country.

Surf's up...

Presidential elections are the "Super Bowls" of our electoral system. Learn more about these great events at the following sites:

fec.gov/pages/ecworks.htm

learning.loc.gov/learn/election/elecprocess.html

fec.gov/pages/elecvote.htm

The electors arrive at their state capital on the first Monday after the second Wednesday in December to cast their ballots. These ballots are then sent to Congress, and early in January, Congress formally counts the ballots and declares what everybody already watched on television—who won the election for president and vice president.

The following table shows the number of electoral votes awarded to each state. To win a presidential election, a candidate must earn 270 electoral votes, which means winning in the most populated states, such as Texas and California. For example, together California and Texas have 89 electoral votes; this is more than Alabama, Alaska, Arkansas, Colorado, Connecticut, Delaware, Georgia, Hawaii, Idaho, Iowa, Kentucky, and Louisiana combined!

State	Electoral Votes
Alabama	9
Alaska	3
Arizona	10
Arkansas	6
California	55
Colorado	9
Connecticut	7
Delaware	3
District of Columbia	3
Florida	27
Georgia	15
Hawaii	4
Idaho	4
Illinois	21
Indiana	11
Iowa	7
Kansas	6
Kentucky	8
Louisiana	9
Maine	4

State	Electoral Votes
Maryland	10
Massachusetts	12
Michigan	17
Minnesota	10
Mississippi	6
Missouri	11
Montana	3
Nebraska	5
Nevada	5
New Hampshire	4
New Jersey	15
New Mexico	5
New York	31
North Carolina	15
North Dakota	3
Ohio	20
Oklahoma	7
Oregon	7
Pennsylvania	21
Rhode Island	4
South Carolina	8
South Dakota	3
Tennessee	11
Texas	34
Utah	5

State	Electoral Votes
Vermont	3
Virginia	13
Washington	11
West Virginia	5
Wisconsin	10
Wyoming	3
Total	538

It takes a majority of the electoral votes to win. If no candidate earns a majority of the electoral votes for president, the House chooses among the top three candidates with each group of state representatives having one vote. If no candidate gets a majority of the electoral votes for vice president, the Senate chooses between the two top candidates with each senator casting one vote.

The Choice Is Yours
Set # 3

To check your understanding of the previous material, answer the following questions by selecting the letter of the correct answer.

1. A campaign strategy involves:
   a. conducting surveys to learn what the voters like and dislike.
   b. buying television time and other advertising to help make the voters aware of their candidate's views and qualifications.
   c. arranging for the candidate to meet with various interest groups and groups of voters.
   d. all of the above.

2. Senators are elected for a term of _____ years.
   a. 3
   b. 2
   c. 6
   d. 4

3. A state's electoral votes are equal to:
   a. the number of senators it has.
   b. a number set by state law.
   c. a number agreed to by both major parties.
   d. the number of its representatives in both houses of Congress.

4. The chart below shows the electoral votes of four different states. State 1 is most likely _____.

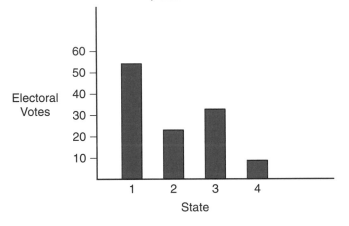

   a. California
   b. North Dakota
   c. Louisiana
   d. Pennsylvania

5. If no presidential candidate earns a majority of electoral votes, the _____ chooses among the top three candidates.
   a. Senate
   b. electoral college
   c. House of Representatives
   d. Supreme Court

CRITICISMS OF OUR ELECTORAL SYSTEM

TV star or leader

Television has become the main method for congressional and presidential candidates to communicate with the voters. Candidates spend less time explaining, in person, their platforms and their qualifications to their potential constituents than they do on television. Many people are concerned that the parties and the voters are selecting candidates based on their "television personalities" rather than on their ability to represent their constituents. Because we have little physical contact with the candidates, we see them only as faces on the television screen. A person may be skilled at problem solving, working with and listening to people, and courageous enough to make difficult decisions, but may not come across well to television viewer voters. Critics of our current system claim that a man such as Abraham Lincoln—quiet, thoughtful and intelligent, but not physically attractive—would find little support from modern voters accustomed to seeing television personality candidates.

The cost of campaigning

The heavy use of television has made modern campaigns expensive. For example, short television advertisements cost as much as $100,000 for a minute! Because "time is money" when it comes to television, candidates must reduce explanations and positions on important issues into slogans. Worse still, many qualified people cannot afford to campaign and many of the candidates must depend on sizable campaign contributions from corporations and powerful special interest groups, which makes them favor

these groups when it comes to legislation. Several possible solutions to the high cost of campaigning have been offered:

- Have the government pay for each candidate's campaign.
- Limit the amount of money that any candidate may spend on a campaign.
- Limit the amount of money that any individual or group may contribute to a campaign.

Recent legislation has been aimed at limiting campaign spending. Federal campaign laws limit the most any individual may give to a candidate in any single election to $2,000. The most that may be given to a *political action committee (PAC)*, which is a special interest group who redistributes the funds to various candidates, is $5,000.

Although federal campaign finance laws have limited direct contributions to candidates, "soft money"—that is, money contributed by individuals and special interest groups to the political party to support the party's position on certain issues—remains unregulated. By law, the party may use the money to advertise about the issues, not the candidates. Nevertheless, the candidates benefit because the voters know their position on the advertised issues. There are no laws regulating contributions used in this manner. Many people are concerned that these contributions will overly influence the candidate once elected to office, and therefore, the candidate will end up representing just a few contributing constituents, rather than all constituents.

Things to Think About

In 1976, in the case of *Buckley v. Valeo*, the Supreme Court ruled that Congress could not limit campaign spending because spending money on politics is a form of constitutionally protected free speech. Today, there are no limits on how much money a candidate or party may spend and no limits on how much a wealthy candidate may donate to his or her own campaign.

1. How is campaign spending a form of free speech?
2. Do wealthy individuals have an unfair advantage in campaigns? If so, how can this be avoided?

Projects You Can Do

1. Learn about the last presidential election. What were some of the issues? Did our electoral system work?
2. Pass your own laws to make campaigns "fair" to all candidates, as well as more informative and meaningful for the voters.
3. Research campaigns by wealthy candidates, such as presidential candidate Steve Forbes and Texas gubernatorial (Governor) candidate Tony Sanchez. Were they successful? If not, why?

SHAPING POLICY

Our government's decisions regarding domestic and foreign policy affect the lives of every citizen. The next chapter looks at how these policies are shaped and by whom.

CHAPTER EIGHT

Shaping Public Policy

PUBLIC POLICY

Thousands of individuals, both inside and outside the national government, help to shape our government's public policy. *Public policy* is our government's actions to solve problems confronting the country. All institutions have policies. For example, your school might have a dress code policy about the kinds of clothes you can wear at school. However, unlike the policies of institutions, such as your school, that address the problems relating only to that institution, public policy must cover a wide range of problems that affect millions of people.

The problems addressed by public policy are not only wide ranging but also difficult to solve for the following reasons:

- The problems are complex, so different people have different ideas on the best way to solve the problems.
- Usually, the policy proposed to solve a problem requires the government to spend a lot of money, and that money comes out of taxes that the citizens pay.
- Our nation is large and complex, so our government must deal with large, complex problems. It might solve one problem, but the solution might make another problem worse, or it may create a new problem. For example, government policy makers might decide to improve our roads by repairing the old ones and building new ones. Unfortunately, this course of action uses money that could have been used to improve schools.

Projects You Can Do

1. Ask an adult family member about how he or she decides what to spend money on. What is your family's "economic policy"?
2. Ask your teacher to explain some of your school's policies. Who makes your school's policies? Are certain groups of people able to influence your school's policy makers? Who are they? How do they make their views known?

3. Develop your own policy to address one of the following problems facing our country:
   - hunger
   - air pollution
   - lack of adequate parks and recreational areas.

Regardless of these difficulties, shaping public policy is an important responsibility of our government. Policy makers must obtain a *consensus* or agreement among various groups who influence public policy in order to develop a policy that benefits our country. To understand the policy-making process, let's first see who influences public policy and the policy makers.

INFLUENCE OVER PUBLIC POLICY

Depending on the problem being considered, one or more of the following groups will try to influence the policy makers to create a policy solution favorable to their group.

Special interest groups

A *special interest group* is an organized group of people who are committed to a cause and who attempt to persuade policy makers to develop public policy that supports that cause. This persuasion is attempted through the following techniques:

- *Lobbying* is meeting personally with legislators and other policy makers to try to convince them to vote in a certain way or to introduce legislation that supports the special interest group's position. *Lobbyists* (those people representing special interest groups and their cause who lobby policy makers) depend on their personal relationship with members of Congress and the executive branch to accomplish their goals.

- Contributing money to the campaigns of candidates who support the special interest group's cause.
- Advertising in the media to inform the public and the policy makers about their cause and the public policy they favor.

These techniques can be quite effective, and special interest groups don't always support popular views. As a result, the efforts of a special interest group can sometimes create a policy that is opposed by a majority of Americans. An example is gun control. An overwhelming number of Americans favor some type of gun control; however, special interest groups who oppose it continue to work harder to ensure their opinion remains our government's public policy on gun control.

Surf's up...

Glide onto these sites to learn more about two special interest groups: (1) Mothers Against Drunk Drivers and (2) Greenpeace.

madd.org/home/

greenpeace.org/homepage/

The media

The *media* includes newspapers, magazines, radio, television, and the Internet. The media provides a constant flow of news and analysis; therefore, Americans, especially the policy makers, have a tremendous amount of information available to them about issues and problems confronting our country. The owners of media companies can focus the attention of viewers on particular policy problems, thus influencing both the public and the policy makers regarding those issues. This means that media organizations enjoy various methods of indirect influence over policy decisions.

The public

An individual's background influences his or her opinion on issues and on general political views. *Public opinion* refers to opinions and feelings that we hold on important issues facing our country. Policy makers use public opinion to understand how the people they represent feel about certain issues and problems. Therefore, it is important for policy makers to be able to accurately determine public opinion.

Accurate measurement of public opinion is accomplished through *public opinion polls*, which are telephone or mail questionnaires used to determine the number of people who hold a certain opinion on an issue of interest to policy makers.

Did You Know?

Opinion polls have been a valuable tool for policy makers since the 1930s, when George Gallup first developed techniques to accurately measure the opinions of a large number of people.

Things to Think About

1. How does a special interest group, such as Mothers Against Drunk Drivers, try to influence public opinion? Have they been successful?
2. How do the various forms of media attempt to influence public policy? Which methods seem the most effective? Why?

We've seen the groups who have an interest in trying to influence public policy. Now, let's learn about the policy makers they are trying to influence.

THE POLICY MAKERS

Congress

Congress can create policy by passing one or more new laws.
The process, at times, can be complex. Sometimes what we
think of as a single policy is really a bundle of several laws or
amendments to laws. Special interest groups, the media, and the
public attempt to influence this legislative process by providing
information that will cause the legislators to hold similar opinions on particular issues. Gaining an agreement of opinions from
the legislators and other policy makers is necessary for creating
public policy.

The president and the executive bureaucracy

As with Congress, the president is influenced by various groups
regarding public policy. The president can shape public policy
by:

- mentioning an issue or problem, as well as suggesting the
  policy to solve it in speeches, such as the State of the Union
  Address. (Refer to Chapter Five for a discussion on the State
  of the Union Address.)
- funding a proposed policy in the annual budget.
- vetoing a law that Congress passed. Because a law or group of
  laws can serve as a policy, the veto of a law or laws has the effect of creating a new policy.
- issuing an executive order, which can act as a policy.

The executive bureaucracy, discussed in Chapter Five, contains policy makers, as well. These agencies and people who assist the president suggest strategies and propose laws that can
become policy.

The judicial branch

As mentioned in Chapter One, a successful representative democracy must protect the views of the minority. One way our representative democracy does this is through our judicial system. As we saw in Chapter Six, the judicial system is headed by the Supreme Court, which has been effective in protecting minority viewpoint rights. For example, most Americans prefer laws banning flag burning. Nevertheless, the Supreme Court, time after time, has ruled that any legislation prohibiting flag burning would violate the constitutional rights of the small group of people desiring to protest in this manner.

A Minute with Senator WordSmart
Set # 1

Take a minute to make sure that you understand the meanings of the new words. Match the word in the left-hand column with its definition in the right-hand column by drawing a line from the word to its definition. If you want to check your work, refer to the Answer Key in the back of the book.

1. Public policy

2. Consensus

3. Special interest groups

a. Newspapers, magazines, radio, television, and the Internet.

b. Organized groups of people who are committed to their beliefs and attempt to persuade policy makers to develop public policy to support those beliefs.

c. Those people who represent special interest groups and their cause and lobby policy makers.

4. Lobbying

    d. Personally meeting with legislators and other policy makers to attempt to convince them to vote in a certain way or to introduce legislation that supports the special interest group's position.

5. Lobbyists

    e. Telephone or mail surveys used to determine the number of people who hold a certain opinion on an issue of interest to policy makers.

6. Media

    f. Refers to opinions and feelings that we hold on important issues facing our country.

7. Public opinion

    g. Our government's actions to solve problems confronting the country.

8. Public opinion polls

    h. Agreement.

We've learned about the policy makers and the people who try to influence them. Now, let's look at the policy-making process.

THE POLICY-MAKING PROCESS

Step 1. Determining the problem

When a special interest group, the media, or some citizens identify a problem they feel needs solving, they typically introduce that problem to certain policy makers. Once one or more policy makers agree that the suggested policy would be beneficial, the problem is brought to the public's attention, and through opinion polls, the policy makers determine how the public views the problem. For example, let's assume that certain members of Congress feel that the large number of homeless people in the large cities needs to be reduced. Through opinion polls and talking with fellow government officials and civic leaders, they learn that many others feel the same way.

Step 2. Developing a policy

The policy makers discuss the problem and try to agree on a policy to solve it. Developing a policy might involve passing new laws, starting a new social or economic program, or developing a plan of action to deal with another country.

Continuing with our example to address the plight of the homeless: Congress passes legislation that creates homes for the homeless. This policy distributes federal funds to cities so that local governments can coordinate the building of homes for the homeless to live in, free of charge.

Step 3. Carrying out the policy

Where necessary, various groups and agencies within the national, state, and local governments are given the responsibility to make the policy work. They establish procedures for running the programs, usually in the form of regulations, specialized training, or education. In our example, local governments in large cities would establish agencies within their government to coordinate the building of the homes and to help place the homeless in them. These agencies will be completely funded by the homes-for-the-homeless legislation.

Step 4. Evaluating the policy

After the policy has been operating for a period, groups and individuals inside and outside the government determine if the policy is addressing the problem. They do this by checking to see if the goals of the policy are being met. If the policy isn't achieving the desired results, they recommend changes to improve the situation.

Suppose, in our example, that civic leaders are satisfied with the number and quality of the homes. A goal for the number of homes and the type had been set during the policy-making process, and that goal has been achieved. They have determined, however, that many of the homeless who might want to take advantage of the program are unaware of the program. The policy makers respond by adding another program that will fund additional city staff to visit areas where the homeless congregate and inform them, in person, of the available homes.

The Choice Is Yours
Set # 1

To check your understanding of the previous material, answer the following questions by selecting the letter of the correct answer. If you want to check your work, refer to the Answer Key in the back of the book.

1. An area on which a special interest group might concentrate its efforts is _____.
   a. enforcing gun control
   b. protecting the environment
   c. aiding immigrants from the Middle East
   d. all of the above

2. The rights and opinion of the minority regarding an issue are most often protected by _____.
   a. the judicial system
   b. Congress
   c. the public
   d. the president

3. Problems addressed by public policy are often difficult to solve because _____.
   a. many people might not agree that it is a problem
   b. solving the problem will cost a lot of money
   c. opinions regarding how the problem should be solved vary
   d. all of the above

4. The following is not an example of a problem that might be addressed by public policy:
   a. U.S. relations with China
   b. Employment opportunities in the United States
   c. Cost of ice cream in New York City middle school cafeterias
   d. Adequate health care for elderly Americans

5. The following are the steps (in their correct order) used in the policy-making process:
   a. Developing a policy, determining the problem, evaluating the policy, and carrying out the policy
   b. Evaluating the policy, developing a policy, carrying out the policy, and determining the problem
   c. Determining the problem, developing a policy, carrying out the policy, and evaluating the policy
   d. Determining the problem, evaluating the policy, developing a policy, and carrying out the policy

TYPES OF PUBLIC POLICY

We've seen who influences and makes our country's public policy, as well as the process for creating and carrying it out. Next, let's look at the different types of policy that make up public policy. Our country's public policy falls into two broad categories: domestic policy and foreign policy.

Domestic policy

Domestic policy refers to the actions that our government policy makers take to solve social and economic problems occurring within the United States. Our government's domestic policy typically attempts to solve various social and economic problems by encouraging or discouraging behaviors. For example, many feel that a well-educated population is needed to help our country prosper and to run our government. Consequently, one domestic policy is to provide free public schooling for elementary-, middle-, and high-school students. The government also provides low-interest loans to help some high-school graduates afford college.

On the other hand, government, through domestic policy, will discourage behavior that it considers undesirable. For example, current domestic policy tries to prevent illegal drug use among citizens by arresting people who sell or use illegal drugs. The goal of the policy is to discourage other citizens from becoming involved with illegal drugs.

We can further divide domestic policy into social policy and economic policy. *Social policy* deals with the actions our government policy makers take to improve the quality of life for Americans. Although social policy covers a wide variety of topics, the most challenging social policy areas are:

- public assistance (helping the poor and disabled)
- health care
- education
- Social Security.

All of these policy areas provide benefits to some or all citizens; however, we must also find a way to pay for these benefits. Consequently, it is this balancing of costs and benefits that causes disagreements among various groups. Nevertheless, it is out of these disagreements that a social policy must be created and carried out. Let's take a quick look at the main areas of social policy:

Public assistance

Public assistance is a social policy consisting of a group of programs that have been established by the government to help the poor and disabled. Over the past few decades, the policy has added programs that provide payments and services to the poor, the unemployed, and the disabled in the form of job training, money contributions for food and housing, free school lunches, and limited medical care.

Health care

A problem facing our country is that many people have little or no health care. Our citizens will have better lives if they can go to the doctor when they are sick as well as when they seek preventive care. Unfortunately, health care costs have risen dramatically over the past ten years. Policy makers would like every person to have quality health care, but they disagree on who

247

should pay the costs of providing health care for those who cannot afford it, so this portion of the problem remains unresolved.

Education

As mentioned earlier, educating our citizens is one of the government's most important social policies. Current policy assigns much of the responsibility of educating young people to the state and local governments. Nevertheless, the federal government plays an important role in shaping this social policy by funding public schools, providing low-interest college loans to high school graduates, and establishing national goals for better education.

Surf's up...

To learn more about some of our country's social policies, check out these web sites:

os.dhhs.gov (Department of Health and Human Services)

ed.gov (Department of Education)

Social Security

Social Security is a social policy consisting of a combination of programs to help the elderly and disabled. These programs provide retirement benefits, health insurance, and support for disabled workers and the children of deceased or disabled workers. Begun in 1935 with the Social Security Act and part of President Franklin Roosevelt's New Deal, Social Security is perhaps the most significant social policy in U.S. history. Under the Social Security program, employers deduct money from the paychecks of their employees, match it with an equal amount of their own money, and then send it to the federal government to provide funds for the various programs. Social Security uses the money paid by today's workers to help cover the needs of today's elderly and disabled.

Antiterrorism efforts

Since September 11, 2001, the United States has been constantly on guard against terrorism, and fighting terrorism has become an important social policy. We have developed and are now evaluating our policy to effectively deal with terrorism, while at the same time protecting the civil liberties of our citizens, which were discussed in Chapter Three. The Department of Homeland Security, a part of the executive Bureaucracy, heads this social policy. This department provides funding and assignments to national, state, and local organizations involved in protecting our citizens from terrorism.

Surf's up...

This site will help you learn more about the Department of Homeland Security and our county's social policy regarding terrorism:

dhs.gov/dhspublic/index.jsp

Things to Think About

1. Should Americans be responsible for their own "social security"? That is, should policy makers not concern themselves about the elderly and disabled? Should these groups be responsible for saving all the money that they need for their retirement years?
2. To keep health care costs from rising so much, should the policy makers adopt a policy and pass legislation that prohibits doctors and hospitals from raising their fees? What are the good points of this proposal? What are the bad points?
3. Who should pay for the cost of protecting the citizens from terrorism? Should it be the national government, state and local governments, or some combination?

Economic policy

Economic policy includes programs and actions taken by government policy makers to create a strong economy that benefits all Americans. To maintain a strong economy, the national government seeks to accomplish three policy goals:

- to ensure reasonable prices for goods and services
- to have jobs available for people who want jobs
- to provide economic growth that leads to improved economic conditions for all citizens.

An example of economic policy might be that policy makers have determined that they need to do more to help American car makers because doing so would promote economic growth. Consequently, a policy is developed, and Congress passes legislation that allows anyone who purchases an American-made car a $500 deduction on the income tax bill (the amount of money a person owes the government based on the amount of money earned during the previous year). The car companies advertise this savings to potential customers, and individual legislators inform their constituents. After six months, the policy is evaluated through opinion polls and car dealers' records. The policy makers are informed that car sales have increased substantially; thus, the policy is determined to be successful.

Surf's up...

The Federal Reserve Board, which is part of the executive branch, is one of the main policy makers of economic policy. Check out their site to learn more about this important group of policy makers:

federalreserve.gov/

A Minute with Senator WordSmart
Set # 2

Match the word in the left-hand column with its definition in the right-hand column.

1. Domestic policy

2. Social policy

3. Public assistance

4. Social Security

5. Economic policy

a. A social policy consisting of a combination of programs funded through taxes paid by employers and employees to help the elderly and disabled.

b. The programs and actions taken by the government policy makers to create a strong economy that benefits all Americans.

c. A social policy consisting of a group of programs established by the government to help the poor and disabled.

d. Deals with actions our government policy makers take to improve the quality of life for Americans.

e. Refers to the actions taken by our government's policy makers to solve social and economic problems occurring within the United States.

Foreign policy

The other main category of public policy is foreign policy. *Foreign policy* is a national government's practices and procedures for dealing with other countries. The main objective of our country's foreign policy is to maintain our independence and freedom. Policy makers also want to promote democracy, as well as encourage economic and social relationships with other countries in such areas as the air and water pollution, develop markets for our products, and prevent illegal drugs from entering our country.

Effective foreign policy requires time, money, and effort. We need to keep our *embassies* (the official U.S. office in a foreign country) open and our people trained so that they can maintain friendly relations with other countries, provide financial aid to countries that need it, and address the threats of terrorism and international crime.

Foreign policy makers

CONGRESS

Congress, because of its many powers, has an important role as a foreign policy maker. For example, the Senate has the power to approve treaties with foreign countries and to approve presidential appointments for ambassadors. Also, Congress has the constitutional power to declare war and approve payments to foreign aid programs.

THE PRESIDENT AND THE EXECUTIVE BUREAUCRACY

Although Congress has this important role in shaping foreign policy, the president (with the aid of the entire executive bureaucracy) is the chief foreign policy maker. The operations of foreign policy are directly under supervision of the president. Also, presidents are more likely to set foreign policy objectives because of the inherent powers that come with their important job and their opportunities to communicate directly with foreign leaders and the American public. (Refer to Chapter Five for more about the president's inherent powers related to foreign policy.)

Carrying out of foreign policy

Several methods are available to carry out our nation's foreign policy:

- diplomacy
- foreign aid
- economic sanctions
- military force.

Diplomacy is the process of developing a relationship with another country so that both countries can discuss important issues. The United States has diplomatic relations with most nations in the world.

Foreign aid is money and services provided to a country to help it care for the social and economic needs of its citizens. The United States provides foreign aid to several financially poor African countries and, most recently, Iraq, to help these countries whose economies have been hurt by such things as famine and war.

Economic sanctions are economic penalties that the United States imposes on countries that threaten our national security or the national security of our *allies* (countries that, through treaties, we have promised to protect). These sanctions may include not doing business with the country, stopping the threatening country from doing business with other countries, and not permitting any U.S. citizen to travel to the country. The United States currently has economic sanctions in force against Cuba.

Military force is the last resort. If our security is threatened and all other methods have failed, we will use our military to protect our allies or ourselves and try to compel the other nation to change its foreign policy toward our allies or us. Most recently, the United States has used military force against Iraq and terrorist groups in Afghanistan.

Creating foreign policy follows the same steps as the process for creating all public policy:

- determining the problem
- developing a policy
- carrying out the policy
- evaluating the policy.

For example, policy makers might determine that our interests would be better protected if another country couldn't threaten us with nuclear weapons. Therefore, our foreign policy makers develop policy that begins with diplomacy. We try to convince the threatening nation to get rid of its nuclear weapons. If that doesn't accomplish our goal, policy makers may choose to impose economic sanctions against the country. If threatening the country causes it to disarm, we would declare the policy successful. If it does not, we would attempt to develop a new policy, possibly considering more-serious measures.

Surf's up...

To learn more about our country's foreign relations policy, check out the site for the U.S. Senate Committee on Foreign Relations:

senate.gov/~foreign/

A Minute with Senator WordSmart
Set # 3

Match the word in the left-hand column with its definition in the right-hand column.

1. Foreign policy

2. Embassy

3. Diplomacy

4. Foreign aid

5. Economic sanctions

6. Allies

7. Military force

a. The process of developing a relationship with another country so that both countries can discuss issues.

b. Penalties imposed by the United States on countries that oppose us on matters involving our security or the security of one or more of our allies.

c. To use our military to protect our allies or ourselves and try to compel the other nation to change its policy toward our allies or us.

d. A national government's practices and procedures for dealing with other countries.

e. Countries that, through treaties, we have agreed to protect.

f. The official office of the United States in a foreign country.

g. Financial aid to a country to help it care for the social and economic needs of its citizens.

The Choice Is Yours
Set # 2

To check your understanding of the previous material, answer the following questions by selecting the letter of the correct answer.

1. Which is not an example of domestic policy?
   a. Sending troops to the Persian Gulf
   b. Increasing the money available for public assistance
   c. Encouraging the unemployed to take advantage of government-funded job training
   d. Using tax money to build a new highway from Florida to Maine

2. Which is an example of economic policy?
   a. Creating a Department of Homeland Security
   b. Making a new treaty with Japan
   c. Sending diplomats to a newly-created foreign country.
   d. Lowering income taxes.

3. Which is not an example of foreign policy?
   a. Refusing to import steel from Japan
   b. Encouraging people to vacation in England
   c. Lowering taxes
   d. Signing a treaty with China

4. Which policymaker is most likely to influence foreign policy?
   a. The president
   b. Congress
   c. The public
   d. The media

5. Which is a method of implementing foreign policy?
   a. Sending troops into a foreign country
   b. Refusing to buy a country's products
   c. The president traveling to a foreign country to meet with its leaders
   d. All of the above

Projects You Can Do

Use your local library or the Internet to:

1. Learn about our foreign policy toward a country of interest to you. Is the policy a "friendly" one? If so, why? If not, why? Has our foreign policy toward this country changed over the last ten years? If it has, why?
2. Learn about which countries the United States has used economic sanctions against. Were they effective? Why or why not?
3. Understand the problems associated with one of the following social policies:
   - public assistance
   - health care
   - education
   - Social Security
   - fighting terrorism.

What you can do

We have learned how our government was formed and how it functions. The important question remains: What can *you* do to make our government better, and to help it serve all Americans? The final chapter explores some things that you can do.

CHAPTER NINE

What You Can Do

WORKING TO KEEP YOUR FREEDOM

Some Americans take their freedom for granted, thinking that because they were born free, they will remain free. Unfortunately, this is not the case. Freedom requires good citizenship. A free nation whose citizens refuse to accept their responsibilities as citizens risk losing their freedom to a small self-interested group who may take control. Let's look at how you can carry out your responsibilities as a citizen in this country.

FOLLOWING YOUR RESPONSIBILITIES AS A CITIZEN

Staying Informed

For our government to represent us effectively, we must be able to inform our representatives about the policies we prefer. Therefore, the first step to good citizenship is understanding the problems confronting our nation and how these problems should be addressed in our representative democracy. To be informed, you can:

- read newspapers and magazines that discuss the issues confronting our country

- listen to speeches made by your legislators and the president
- read the information posted on Web sites maintained by your representatives

- continue to learn about our system of government by taking a course in school and reading books on the subject.

STAYING INVOLVED

Voting is one of the most important ways a person can stay involved in our government. Does this mean that if you are too young to vote, there is nothing for you to do? No. As an informed citizen, you can involve yourself by:

- writing to your legislators and letting them know your opinion on important issues
- helping, if you can, in the campaigns of candidates who support your views on important issues

- informing people who are old enough to vote about important issues
- with your parents' permission, joining a special interest group that supports a goal that is important to you

ENCOURAGING OTHERS TO LEARN AND PARTICIPATE

Ours is a representative democracy. That means, the more people who are informed and involved in the governing process, the better our representatives can represent us. Therefore, you need to encourage others to learn about our government and understand the issues confronting it. Talk to your friends about issues facing our country. Inform them who their representatives are and how they can make their views known to their representatives.

Our government is constantly changing. The ideals remain the same, but the problems and the people change. To keep our country independent and prosperous, our government will have to meet many challenges. It is up to you as a citizen of our next generation of leaders to be ready to take your leadership position in our system. Good government begins with you.

FURTHER READING

Barbour, Christine and Gerald Wright. *Keeping the Republic*. New York: Houghton Mifflin, 2001.

Commager, Henry Steele and Allan Nevins. *Pocket History of the United States*. New York: Pocket Books, 1992.

Cronin, Thomas E., James Burns, and J. W. Peltason, and David Magleby. *Government by the People*, 18th ed. Upper Saddle River, N.J.: Prentice Hall, 2000.

Ginsberg, Benjamin, Theodore Lowi, and Kenneth Shepsle. *American Government*, 7th ed. New York: W.W. Norton & Co., 2002.

Lader, Curt, *How to Prepare for the U.S. Government and Politics Advanced Placement Examination*, 3rd ed. Hauppauge, N.Y.: Barron's Educational Series, 2002.

APPENDIX

A. THE CONSTITUTION OF THE UNITED STATES

PREAMBLE

We the People of the United States, in Order to form a more perfect Union, establish Justice, insure domestic Tranquility, provide for the common defense, promote the general Welfare, and secure the Blessings of Liberty to ourselves and our Posterity, do ordain and establish the Constitution of the United States of America.

ARTICLE I.

Section 1. All legislative Powers herein granted shall be vested in a Congress of the United States, which shall consist of a Senate and House of Representatives.

Section 2. [1] The House of Representatives shall be composed of Members chosen every second Year by the People of the several States, and the Electors in each State shall have the Qualifications requisite for Electors of the most numerous Branch of the State Legislature.
[2] No Person shall be a Representative who shall not have attained to the Age of twenty-five Years, and been seven Years a Citizen of the United States, and who shall not, when elected, be an Inhabitant of that State in which he shall be chosen.
[3] Representatives and direct Taxes shall be apportioned among the several States which may be included within this Union, according to their respective Numbers, which shall be determined by adding to the whole Number of free Persons, including those bound to Service for a Term of Years, and excluding Indians not taxed, three-fifths of all other persons. The actual Enumeration shall be made within three Years after the first Meeting of the Congress of the United States, and within every subsequent Term of ten Years, in such Manner as they shall by Law direct. The Number of Representatives shall not exceed one for every thirty Thousand, but each State shall have at Least one Representative: and until such enumeration shall be made, the State of New Hampshire shall be entitled to choose three, Massachusetts eight, Rhode Island and Providence Plantations one, Connecticut five, New York six, New Jersey four, Pennsylvania

eight, Delaware one, Maryland six, Virginia ten, North Carolina five, South Carolina five, and Georgia three.

[4] When vacancies happen in the Representation from any State, the Executive Authority thereof shall issue Writs of Election to fill such Vacancies.

[5] The House of Representatives shall choose their Speaker and other Officers; and shall have the sole Power of Impeachment.

Section 3. [1] The Senate of the United States shall be composed of two Senators from each State, chosen by the Legislature thereof, for six Years; and each Senator shall have one Vote.

[2] Immediately after they shall be assembled in Consequence of the first Election, they shall be divided as equally as may be into three Classes. The Seats of the Senators of the first Class shall be vacated at the Expiration of the Second Year, of the second Class at the Expiration of the fourth Year, and of the third Class at the Expiration of the sixth Year, so that one-third may be chosen every second Year; and if Vacancies happen by Resignation, or otherwise, during the Recess of the Legislature of any State, the Executive thereof may make temporary Appointments until the next Meeting of the Legislature, which shall then fill such Vacancies.

[3] No Person shall be a Senator who shall have not attained to the Age of thirty Years, and been nine Years a citizen of the United States, and who shall not, when elected, be an inhabitant of that State for which he shall be chosen.

[4] The Vice President of the United States shall be President of the Senate, but shall have no Vote, unless they be equally divided.

[5] The Senate shall choose their other Officers, and also a President pro tempore, in the Absence of the Vice President, or when he shall exercise the Office of President of the United States.

[6] The Senate shall have the sole Power to try all impeachments. When sitting for that Purpose, they shall be on Oath or Affirmation. When the President of the United States is tried, the Chief Justice shall preside: And no Person shall be convicted without the Concurrence of two-thirds of the Members present.

[7] Judgment in Cases of Impeachment shall not extend further than to removal from Office, and disqualification to hold and enjoy any Office of honor, Trust, or Profit under the United States, but the Party convicted shall nevertheless be liable and subject to Indictment, Trial, Judgment, and Punishment, according to Law.

Section 4. [1] The times, Places and Manner of holding Elections for Senators and Representatives shall be prescribed in each State by the Legislature thereof; but the Congress may at any time by Law make or alter such Regulations, except as to the Places of choosing Senators.

[2] The Congress shall assemble at least once every Year, and such Meeting shall be on the first Monday in December, unless they shall by Law appoint a different Day.

Section 5. [1] Each House shall be the Judge of the Elections, Returns, and Qualifications of its own Members, and a Majority of each shall constitute a Quorum to do Business; but a smaller Number may adjourn from day to day, and may be authorized to compel the Attendance of absent Members, in such Manner, and under such Penalties as each House may provide.

[2] Each House may determine the Rules of its Proceedings, punish its Members for disorderly Behavior, and with the Concurrence of two-thirds, expel a Member.

[3] Each house shall keep a Journal of its Proceedings, and for time to time publish the same, excepting such Parts as may in their Judgment require Secrecy; and the Yeas and Nays of the Members of either House on any question shall, at the Desire of one-fifth of these Present, be entered on the Journal.

[4] Neither House, during the Session of Congress, shall, without the Consent of the other, adjourn for more than three days, nor to any other Place than that in which the two Houses shall be sitting.

Section 6. [1] The Senators and Representatives shall receive a Compensation for their Services, to be ascertained by Law, and paid out of the Treasury of the United States. They shall in all Cases, except Treason, Felony and Breach of the Peace, be privileged from Arrest during their Attendance at the Session of their respective Houses, and in going to and returning from the same; and for any Speech or Debate in either House, they shall not be questioned in any other Place.

[2] No Senator or Representative shall, during the Time for which he was elected, be appointed to any civil Office under the Authority of the United States, which shall have been created, or the Emoluments whereof shall have been increased during such time and no Person holding any Office under the United States, shall be a Member of either House during his Continuance in Office.

Section 7. [1] All Bills of raising Revenue shall originate in the House of Representatives; but the Senate may propose or concur with Amendments as on other Bills.

[2] Every Bill which shall have passed the House of Representatives and the Senate, shall, before it becomes a Law, be presented to the President of the United States; if he approves, he shall sign it, but if not he shall return it, with his Objections to the House in which it shall have originated, who shall enter the Objections at large on their Journal, and proceed to

reconsider it. If after such Reconsideration two-thirds of that House shall agree to pass the Bill, it shall be sent together with the Objections, to the other House, by which it shall likewise be reconsidered, and if approved by two-thirds of that House, it shall become Law. But in all such Cases the Votes of both Houses shall be determined by Yeas and Nays, and the Names of the Persons voting for and against the Bill shall be entered on the Journal of each House respectively. If any Bill shall not be returned by the President within ten Days (Sundays excepted) after it shall have been presented to him, the Same shall be a Law, in like Manner as if he had signed it, unless the Congress by their Adjournment prevents its Return, in which Case it shall not be a Law.

[3] Every Order, Resolution, or Vote to which the Concurrence of the Senate and House of Representatives may be necessary (except on a question of Adjournment) shall be presented to the President of the United States; and before the Same shall take Effect, shall be approved by him, or being disapproved by him, shall be repassed by two-thirds of the Senate and House of Representatives, according to the Rules and Limitations prescribed in the Case of a Bill.

Section 8. [1] The Congress shall have the power To lay and collect Taxes, Duties, Imposts, and Excises, to pay the Debts and pro-vide for the common Defense and general Welfare of the United States; but all Duties, Imposts and Excises shall be uniform throughout the United States;

[2] To borrow money on the credit of the United States

[3] To regulate Commerce with foreign Nations, and among the several States, and with the Indian Tribes;

[4] To establish a uniform Rule of Naturalization, and uniform Laws on the subject of Bankruptcies throughout the United States;

[5] To coin Money, regulate the Value thereof, and of foreign coin, and fix the Standard of Weights and Measures;

[6] To provide for the Punishment of counterfeiting the Securities and current Coin of the United States;

[7] To Establish Post Offices and post Roads;

[8] To promote the Progress of Science and useful Arts, be securing for limited times to Authors and Inventors the exclusive Right to their respective Writings and Discoveries;

[9] To constitute Tribunals inferior to the supreme Court;

[10] To define and punish Piracies and Felonies committed on the high Seas, and Offenses against the Law of Nations;

[11] To declare War, grant Letters of Marque and Reprisal, and make Rules concerning Captures on Land and Water;

[12] To raise and support Armies, but no Appropriation of

Money to that Use shall be for a longer Term than two Years;

[13] To provide and maintain a Navy;

[14] To make Rules for the Government and Regulation of the land and naval Forces;

[15] To provide for calling forth the Militia to execute the Laws of the Union, suppress insurrections and repel Invasions;

[16] To provide for organizing, arming, and disciplining, the Militia, and for governing such Part of them as may be employed in the Service of the United States, reserving to the States respectively, the Appointment of the Officers, and the Authority of training the Militia according to the discipline prescribed by Congress;

[17] To exercise exclusive Legislation in all Cases whatsoever, over such District (not exceeding ten Miles square) as may, by Cession of particular States, and the Acceptance of Congress, become the seat of the Government of the United States, and to exercise the Authority over all Places purchased by the Consent of the Legislature of the State in which the Same shall be, for the Erection of Forts, Magazines, Arsenals, dock-Yards, and other needful Buildings; And

[18] To make all Laws which shall be necessary and proper for carrying into Execution the foregoing Powers, and all other Powers vested by the Constitution in the Government of the United States, or in any Department or Officer thereof.

Section 9. [1] The Migration and Importation of Such Persons as any of the States now existing shall think proper to admit, shall not be prohibited by the Congress prior to the Year one thousand eight hundred and eight, but a Tax or duty may be imposed on such importation, not exceeding ten dollars for each Person.

[2] The privilege of the Writ of Habeas Corpus shall not be suspended, unless when in Cases of Rebellion or Invasion the public Safety may require it.

[3] No Bill of Attainder or ex post facto Laws shall be passed.

[4] No Capitation, or other direct, Tax shall be laid, unless in Proportion to the Census or Enumeration herein before directed to be taken.

[5] No Tax or Duty shall be laid on Articles exported from any State.

[6] No Preference shall be given by any Regulation of Commerce or Revenue to the Ports of one State over those of another; nor shall Vessels bound to, or from, one State be obliged to enter, clear, or pay Duties in another.

[7] No money shall be drawn from the Treasury, but in Consequence of Appropriations made by Law; and a regular Statement and Account of the Receipts and Expenditures of all public Money shall be published from time to time.

[8] No Title of Nobility shall be granted by the United States: And no Person holding any Office of Profit or Trust under them, shall without the Consent of the

Congress, accept of any present, Emolument, Office, or Title, of any kind whatever, from any King, Prince, or foreign State.

Section 10. [1] No State shall enter into any Treaty, Alliance, or Confederation; grant Letters or Marque and Reprisal; coin Money; emit Bills of Credit; make any thing but gold and silver Coin a Tender in Payment of Debts; pass any Bill of Attainder, ex post facto Law, or Law impairing the Obligation of Contracts, or grant any Title of Nobility.

[2] No State shall, without the Consent of Congress, lay any Imposts or Duties on Imports or Exports, except what may be ab-solutely necessary for executing its inspection Laws; and the net Produce of all Duties and Imposts, laid by any State on Imports or Exports, shall be for the Use of the Treasury of the United States; and all such Laws shall be subject of the Revision and Control of the Congress.

[3] No State shall, without the Consent of Congress, lay any Duty of Tonnage, keep Troops, or Ships of War in time of Peace, enter into any Agreement or Compact with another State, or with a foreign Power, or engage in War, unless actually invaded, or in such immi-nent Danger as will not admit of delay.

ARTICLE II.
Section 1. [1] The executive Power shall be vested in a President of the United States of America. He shall hold his Office during the Term of four Years, and, together with the Vice President, chosen for the same Term, be elected, as follows:

[2] Each State shall appoint, in such Manner as the Legislature thereof may direct, a Number of Electors, equal to the whole Number of Senators and Representatives to which the State may be entitled in Congress; but no Senator or Representative, or Person holding an Office of Trust or Profit under the United States shall be appointed an Elector.

[3] The Electors shall meet in the respective States, and vote by Ballot for two Persons, of whom one at least shall not be an inhabi-tant of the same State with them-selves. And they shall make a List of all the Persons voted for, and of the Number of Votes for each; which List they shall sign and certify, and transmit sealed to the Seal of the Government of the United States, directed to the President of the Senate. The President of the Senate shall, in the presence of the Senate and House of Representatives, open all the Certificates and the Votes shall then be counted. The Person having the greatest Number of Votes shall be the President, if such Number be a Majority of the whole Number of Electors ap-pointed; and if there be more than one who have such Majority, and have an equal Number of Votes, then the House of Representatives shall immediately choose by Ballot one of them for President; and if no Person have a Majority,

then from the five highest on the List the said House shall in like Manner choose the President. But in choosing the President, the Votes shall be taken by States the Representation from each State having one Vote; A quorum for this Purpose shall consist of a Member or Members from two-thirds of the States, and a Majority of all the States shall be necessary to a Choice. In every Case, after the Choice of the President, the Person having the greater Number of Votes of the Electors shall be the Vice President. But if there should remain two or more who have equal votes, the Senate shall choose from them by Ballot the Vice President.

[4] The Congress may determine the Time of choosing the Electors and the Day on which they shall give their Votes; which Day shall be the same throughout the United States.

[5] No Person except a natural born Citizen, or a Citizen of the United States, at the time of the Adoption of this Constitution, shall be eligible to the Office of President; neither shall any Person be eligible to that Office who shall not have attained to the Age of thirty-five Years, and been fourteen Years a Resident within the United States.

[6] In case of the Removal of the President from Office, or of his Death, Resignation or Inability to discharge the Powers and Duties of said Office, the Same shall devolve on the Vice President, and the Congress may by Law provide for the Case of Removal, Death, Resignation or Inability, both of the President and Vice President, declaring what Officer shall then act as President, and such Officer shall act accordingly, until the disability be removed, or a President shall be elected.

[7] The President shall, at stated Times, receive for his Services, a Compensation, which shall neither be increased or diminished during the Period for which he shall have been elected, and he shall not receive within that Period any other Emolument from the United States, or any of them.

[8] Before he enter on the Execution of his Office, he shall take the following Oath or Affirmation: "I do solemnly swear (or affirm) that I will faithfully executed the Office of President of the United States and will to the best of my Ability, preserve, protect and defend the Constitution of the United States."

Section 2. [1] The President shall be Commander in Chief of the Army and Navy of the United States and of the Militia of the several States, when called into the actual Service of the United States; he may require the Opinion, in writing of the principal Officer in each of the executive Departments, upon any Subject relating to the Duties of their respective Offices, and he shall have Power to grant Reprieves and Pardons for Offenses against the United States, except in Cases of Impeachment.

[2] He shall have Power, by and within the Advice and Consent of the Senate to make Treaties, provided two-thirds of the Senators present concur; and he shall nominate, and by and with the Advice and Consent of the Senate, shall appoint Ambassadors, other public Ministers and Consuls, Judges of the supreme Court, and all other Officers of the United States whose Appointments are not herein provided for, and which shall be established by Law, but the Congress may by Law vest the Appointment of such inferior Officers, as they think proper, in the President alone, in the Courts of Law, or in the Heads of Departments.

[3] He shall from time to time give the Congress Information of the State of the Union and recommend to their Consideration such Measures as he shall judge necessary and expedient; he may, on extraordinary Occasions, convene both Houses, or either of them, and in Case of Disagreement between them, with Respect to the Time of Adjournment, he may adjourn them to such Time as he shall think proper; he shall receive Ambassadors and other public Ministers; he shall take Care that the Laws be faithfully executed and shall Commission all the Officers of the United States.

Section 4. The President, Vice President, and all civil Officers of the United States shall be removed from Office on Impeachment for, and Conviction of, Treason, Bribery, or other high Crimes and Misdemeanors.

ARTICLE III.

Section 1. The judicial Power of the United States shall be vested in one supreme Court, and in such inferior Courts as the Congress may from time to time ordain and establish. The Judges, both of the supreme and inferior Courts, shall hold their Offices during good Behavior, and shall, at stated Times, receive for their Services a compensation, which shall not be diminished during their Continuance in Office.

Section 2. [1] The judicial Power shall extend to all Cases, in Law and Equity, arising under this Constitution, the Laws of the United States, and Treaties made, or which shall be made, under their Authority;—to all Cases affecting Ambassadors, other public Ministers and Consuls;—to all Cases of admiralty and maritime Jurisdiction;—to Controversies to which the United States shall be a Party;—between Citizens of different States;—between Citizens of the same State claiming Lands under the Grants of different States, and between a State, or the Citizens thereof, and foreign States, Citizens or Subjects.

[2] In all Cases affecting Ambassadors, other public Ministers and Consuls, and those in which a State shall be a Party, the supreme Court shall have original Jurisdiction. In all other Cases before mentioned, the supreme Court shall have appel-

late Jurisdiction, both as to Law and Fact, with such Exceptions, and under such Regulations as the Congress shall make.

[3] The trial of all Crimes, except in Cases of Impeachment, shall be by Jury; and such Trial shall be held in the State where said Crimes shall have been committed; but when not committed within any State, the Trial shall be at such Place or Places as the Congress may by Law have directed.

Section 3. [1] Treason against the United States shall consist only in levying War against them, or in, adhering to their Enemies, giving them Aid and Comfort. No Person shall be convicted of Treason unless on the Testimony of two Witnesses to the same overt Act, or on Confession in open Court.

[2] Congress shall have the Power to declare the Punishment of Treason, but no Attainder of Treason shall work Corruption of Blood, or Forfeiture except during the Life of the Person attained.

ARTICLE IV.

Section 1. Full Faith and Credit shall be given in each State to the public Acts, Records, and judicial Proceedings of every other State. And the Congress may by general laws prescribe the Manner in which such Acts, Records, and Proceedings shall be proved and the Effect thereof.

Section 2. [1] The Citizens of each State shall be entitled to all Privileges and Immunities of Citizens in the several States.

[2] A person charged in any State with Treason, Felony, or other Crime, who shall flee from Justice, and be found in another State, shall on demand of the executive Authority of the State from which he fled, be delivered up, to be removed to the State having Jurisdiction of the Crime.

[3] No Person held to Service or Labor in one State, under the Laws thereof, escaping into another, shall, in Consequence of any Law or Regulation therein, be discharged from such Service or Labor, but shall be delivered up on Claim of the Party to whom such Service or Labor may be due.

Section 3. [1] New States may be admitted by the Congress into this Union; but no new State shall be formed or erected within the Jurisdiction of any other State; nor any State be formed by the Junction of two or more States, or parts of States, without the consent of the Legislatures of the States concerned as well as of the Congress.

[2] The Congress shall have Power to dispose of and make all needful Rules and Regulations respecting the Territory or other Property belonging to the United States; and nothing in this Constitution shall be so construed as to Prejudice any Claims of the United States, or any particular State.

Section 4. The United States shall guarantee to every State in this Union a Republican Form of Government, and shall protect each of them against Invasion; and on Application of the Legislature, or of the Executive (when the Legislature cannot be convened) against domestic Violence.

ARTICLE V.

The Congress, whenever two-thirds of both Houses shall deem it necessary, shall propose Amendments to this Constitution, or, in the Application of the Legislatures of two-thirds of the several States, shall call a Convention for proposing Amendments, which, in either Case, shall be valid to all Intents and Purposes, as part of this Constitution, when ratified by Legislatures of three-fourths of the several States, or by Conventions in three-fourths thereof, as the one or the other Mode of Ratification may be proposed by the Congress; Provided that no Amendment which may be made prior to the Year One thousand eight hundred and eight shall in any Manner affect the first and fourth Clauses in the Ninth Section of the first Article; and that no State, without its Consent, shall be deprived of its equal Suffrage in the Senate.

ARTICLE VI.

[1] All Debts contracted and Engagements entered into, before the Adoption of this Constitution shall be as valid against the United States under this Constitution, as under the Confederation.

[2] This Constitution, and the laws of the United States which shall be made in Pursuance thereof; and all Treaties made, or which shall be made, under the Authority of the United States, shall be the supreme Law of the Land; and the Judges in every State shall be bound thereby, any thing in the Constitution or Laws of any State to the Contrary notwithstanding.

[3] The Senators and Representatives before mentioned, and the Members of the several State Legislatures, and all executive and judicial Officers, both of the United States and of the several States, shall be bound by Oath and Affirmation, to support this Constitution; but no religious Test shall ever be required as a Qualification to any Office or public Trust under the United States.

ARTICLE VII.

The Ratification of the Conventions of nine States shall be sufficient for the Establishment of this Constitution between the States so ratifying the Same.

B. BILL OF RIGHTS

The conventions of a number of the States having at the time of their adopting the Constitution, expressed a desire, in order to prevent misconstruction or abuse of its powers, that further declaratory and restrictive clauses should be added: And as extending the ground of public confidence in the Government, will best insure the beneficent ends of its institution.

AMENDMENT I.

Congress shall make no law respecting an establishment of religion, or prohibiting the free exercise thereof; or abridging the freedom of speech, or the press; or the right of the people peaceably to assemble, and to petition the Government for a redress of grievances.

AMENDMENT II.

A well-regulated Militia, being necessary to the security of a free State, the right of the people to keep and bear Arms, shall not be infringed.

AMENDMENT III.

No Soldier shall, in time of peace be quartered in any house, without the consent of the Owner, nor in time of war, but in a manner to be prescribed by law.

AMENDMENT IV.

The right of the people to be secure in their persons, houses, papers, and effects, against unreasonable searches and seizures, shall not be violated, and no Warrants shall issue, but upon probable cause, supported by Oath or affirmation, and particularly describing the place to be searched and the persons or things to be seized.

AMENDMENT V.

No person shall be held to answer for a capital, or otherwise infamous crime, unless on a presentment or indictment of a Grand Jury, except in cases arising in the land or naval forces, or in the Militia, when in actual service in time of War or public danger; nor shall any person be subject for the same offence to be twice put in jeopardy of life or limb; nor shall be compelled in any criminal case to be a witness against himself, or be deprived of life, liberty, or property, without due process of law; nor shall private property be taken for public use, without just compensation.

AMENDMENT VI.

In all criminal prosecutions, the accused shall enjoy the right to a speedy and public trial, by an impartial jury of the State and district wherein the crime shall have been committed, which district shall have been previously ascertained by law, and to be informed of the nature and cause of the accusation; to be confronted with the Witnesses against him; to have compulsory process for obtaining witnesses in his favor, and to have the Assistance of Counsel for his defense.

AMENDMENT VII.

In Suits at common law, where the value in controversy shall exceed twenty dollars, the right of trial by jury shall be preserved, and no fact tried by jury, shall be otherwise re-examined in any Court of the United States, than according to the rules of the common law.

AMENDMENT VIII.

Excessive bail shall not be required, nor excessive fines imposed, nor cruel and unusual punishments inflicted.

AMENDMENT IX.

The enumeration in the Constitution, of certain rights, shall not be construed to deny or disparage others retained by the people.

AMENDMENT X.

The powers not delegated to the United States by the Constitution, nor prohibited by it to the States, are reserved to the States respectively, or to the people.

C. DECLARATION OF INDEPENDENCE

When in the Course of human events, it becomes necessary for one people to dissolve the political bonds which have connected them with one another, and to assume the powers of the earth, the separate and equal station to which the Laws of Nature and of Nature's God entitle them, a decent respect to the opinions of mankind requires that they should declare the causes which impel them to the separation.

We hold these truths to be self-evident, that all men are created equal, that they are endowed by their Creator with certain unalienable Rights, that among these are Life, Liberty, and the pursuit of Happiness. That to secure these Rights, Governments are instituted among Men, deriving their just powers from the consent of the governed. That whenever any Form of Government becomes destructive of these ends, it is the Right of the People to alter or abolish it, and to institute new Government, laying its foundations on such principles and organizing its powers in such form, as to them shall seem most likely to effect their Safety and Happiness. Prudence, indeed, will dictate that Governments long established should not be changed for light and transient causes; and accordingly all experience has shown, that mankind are more disposed to suffer, while evils are sufferable, than to right themselves by abolishing the forms to which they are accustomed. But when a long train of abuses and usurpations, pursuing invariably the same Object evinces a design to reduce them under absolute

Despotism, it is their right, it is their duty, to throw off such Government, and to provide new Guards for their future security. Such has been the patient sufferance of these Colonies; and such is now the necessity which constrains them to alter their former Systems of Government, the history of the present King of Great Britain [George III] is a history of repeated injuries and usurpations, all having in direct object the establishment of an absolute Tyranny over these States. To prove this, let Facts be submitted to a candid world.

He has refused his Assent to Laws, the most wholesome and necessary for the public good.

He has forbidden his Governors to pass Laws of immediate and pressing importance unless suspended in their operation till his Assent should be obtained; and when so suspended, he has utterly neglected to attend to them.

He has refused to pass other Laws for the accommodations of large districts of people, unless those people would relinquish the right of Representation in the Legislature, a right inestimable to them and formidable to tyrants only.

He has called together legislative bodies at places unusual, uncomfortable, and distant from the depository of their public Records, for the sole purpose of fatiguing them into compliance with his measures.

He has dissolved Representative Houses repeatedly, for opposing with manly firmness his invasions on the rights of the people.

He has refused for a long time, after such dissolutions, to cause others to be elected; whereby the Legislative powers, incapable of Annihilation, have returned to the People at large for their exercise; the State remaining in the mean time exposed to all the dangers of invasion from without, and convulsions within.

He has endeavored to prevent the population of these States; for that purpose obstructing the laws of Naturalization of Foreigners; refusing to pass others to encourage their migrations hither, and raising the conditions of new Appropriations of Lands.

He has obstructed the Administration of Justice, by refusing his Assent to laws for establishing Judiciary powers.

He has made Judges dependent on his Will alone, for the tenure of their offices, and the amount and payment of their salaries.

He has erected a multitude of New Offices, and sent hither swarms of Officers to harass our people and eat out their substance.

He has kept among us, in times of peace, Standing Armies without the consent of our legislatures.

He has affected to render the Military independent of and superior to Civil power.

He has combined with others to subject us to a jurisdiction foreign to our constitution and unacknowledged by our laws; giving his Assent to their Acts of pretended Legislation.

For quartering large bodies of armed troops among us:

For protecting them, by a mock Trial, from punishment for any Murders which they should commit on the Inhabitants of these States:

For cutting off our Trade with all parts of the world:

For imposing Taxes on us without our Consent:

For depriving us, in many cases, of the benefits of Trial by Jury:

For transporting us beyond Seas to be tried for pretended offenses:

For abolishing the free System of English Laws in a neighboring Province, establishing therein an Arbitrary government, and enlarging its Boundaries so as to render it at once an example and fit instrument for introducing the same absolute rule into these Colonies:

For taking away our Charters, abolishing our most valuable Laws, and altering fundamentally the Forms of our Governments:

For suspending our own Legislatures, and declaring themselves invested with power to legislate for us in all cases whatsoever.

He has abdicated Government here, by declaring us out of his Protection and waging War against us.

He has plundered our seas, ravaged our Coasts, burnt our towns, and destroyed the lives of our people.

He is at this time transporting large Armies of foreign Mercenaries to complete the works of death, desolation, and tyranny, already begun with circumstances of Cruelty and perfidy scarcely paralleled in the most barbarous ages, and totally unworthy the Head of a civilized nation.

He has constrained our fellow Citizens taken Captive on the high Seas to bear Arms against their Country, to become the executioners of their friends and Brethren, or to fall themselves by their Hands.

He has excited domestic insurrections amongst us, and has endeavored to bring on the inhabitants of our frontiers, the merciless Indian Savages, whose known rule of warfare, is an undistinguished destruction of all ages, sexes, and conditions.

In every stage of these Oppressions, We have Petitioned for Redress in the most humble terms: Our repeated Petitions have been answered only by repeated injury. A prince whose character is thus marked by every act which may define a Tyrant, is unfit to be the ruler of free people.

Nor have We been wanting in attention to our British brethren. We have warned them from time to time of attempts by their legislature to extend an unwarrantable jurisdiction over us. We have reminded them of the circumstances of our emigration and settlement here. We have appealed to their native justice and magnanimity, and we have conjured them by the ties of our common kindred to disavow these usurpations, which would inevitably interrupt our connections and correspondence. They too have been deaf to the voice of justice and consanguinity. We must, therefore, acquiesce in the necessity, which denounces our Separation, and hold them, as we hold the rest of mankind, Enemies in War, in Peace, Friends.

We, therefore, the Representatives of the united States of America, in General Congress, Assembled, appealing to the supreme Judge of the world for rectitude of our intentions, do, in the Name, and by the Authority of the good People of these Colonies, solemnly publish and declare, That these United Colonies are, and of Right to be Free and Independent States; that they are Absolved from all Allegiance to the British Crown, and that all political connection between them and the State of Great Britain is and ought to be totally dissolved; and that as Free and Independent States, they have full Power to levy War, conclude Peace, contract Alliances, establish Commerce, and to do all other Acts and Things which Independent States may of right do. And for the support of this Declaration, with a firm reliance on the protection of divine Providence, we mutually pledge to each other our Lives, our Fortunes, and our sacred Honor.

D. ARTICLES OF CONFEDERATION

Articles of Confederation and perpetual Union between the states of New Hampshire, Massachusetts-bay, Rhode Island and Providence Plantations, Connecticut, New York, New Jersey, Pennsylvania, Delaware, Maryland, Virginia, North Carolina, South Carolina, and Georgia.

I.
The Stile of this Confederacy shall be "The United States of America".

II.
Each state retains its sovereignty, freedom, and independence, and every power, jurisdiction, and right, which is not by this Confederation expressly delegated to the United States, in Congress assembled.

III.
The said States hereby severally enter into a firm league of friendship with each other, for their common defense, the security of their liberties, and their mutual and general welfare, binding themselves to assist each other, against all force offered to, or attacks made upon them, or any of them, on account of religion, sovereignty, trade, or any other pretense whatever.

IV.
The better to secure and perpetuate mutual friendship and intercourse among the people of the different States in this Union, the

free inhabitants of each of these States, paupers, vagabonds, and fugitives from justice excepted, shall be entitled to all privileges and immunities of free citizens in the several States; and the people of each State shall have free ingress and regress to and from any other State, and shall enjoy therein all the privileges of trade and commerce, subject to the same duties, impositions, and restrictions as the inhabitants thereof respectively, provided that such restrictions shall not extend so far as to prevent the removal of property imported into any State, of which the owner is an inhabitant; provided also that no imposition, duties or restriction shall be laid by any State, on the property of the United States, or either of them.

If any person guilty of, or charged with, treason, felony, or other high misdemeanor in any State, shall flee from justice, and be found in any of the United States, he shall, upon demand of the Governor or executive power of the State from which he fled, be delivered up and removed to the State having jurisdiction of his offense.

Full faith and credit shall be given in each of these States to the records, acts, and judicial proceedings of the courts and magistrates of every other State.

V.

For the most convenient management of the general interests of the United States, delegates shall be annually appointed in such manner as the legislatures of each State shall direct, to meet in Congress on the first Monday in November, in every year, with a power reserved to each State to recall its delegates, or any of them, at any time within the year, and to send others in their stead for the remainder of the year.

No State shall be represented in Congress by less than two, nor more than seven members; and no person shall be capable of being a delegate for more than three years in any term of six years; nor shall any person, being a delegate be capable of holding any office under the United States, for which he, or another for his benefit, receives any salary fees, or emolument of any kind.

Each State shall maintain its own delegates in a meeting of the States, and while they act as members to the committees of the States.

In determining questions in the United States in Congress assembled, each State shall have one vote. Freedom of speech and debate in Congress shall not be impeached or questioned in any court or place out of Congress, and the members of Congress shall be protected in their persons from arrests or imprisonments, during the time of their going to and from, and attendance on Congress, except for treason, felony, or breach of the peace.

VI.

No State, without the consent of the United States in Congress assembled, shall send any embassy to, or receive any embassy from, or enter into any conference, agreement, alliance, or treaty with any King, Prince, or State; nor shall any person holding any office of profit or trust under the United States, or any of them, accept any present, emolument, office or title of any kind whatever from any King, Prince, or foreign State; nor shall the United States in Congress assembled, or any of them, grant any title of nobility.

No two or more States shall enter into any treaty, confederation or alliance whatever between them, without the consent of the United States in Congress assembled, specifying accurately the purposes for which the same is to be entered into, and how long it shall continue.

No State shall lay any imposts or duties, which may interfere with any stipulations in treaties, entered into by the United States in Congress assembled, with any King, Prince, or State, in pursuance of any treaties already proposed by congress, to the courts of France and Spain.

No vessel of war shall be kept up in time of peace by any State, except such number only, as shall be deemed necessary by the United States in Congress assembled, for the defense of such State, or its trade; nor shall any body of forces be kept up by any State in time of peace, except such number only, as in the judgement of the United States in Congress assembled, shall be deemed requisite to garrison the forts necessary for the defense of such State; but every state shall always keep up a well-regulated and disciplined militia, sufficiently armed and accoutered, and shall provide and constantly have ready for use, in public stores, a due number of field pieces and tents, and a proper quantity of arms, ammunition, and camp equipage.

No State shall engage in any war without the consent of the United States in Congress assembled, unless such State be actually invaded by enemies, or shall have received certain advice of a resolution being formed by some nation of Indians to invade such State, and the danger so imminent as not to admit of a delay till the United States in Congress assembled can be consulted; nor shall any State grant commissions to any ships or vessels of war, nor letters of marque or reprisal, except it be after a declaration of war by the United States in Congress assembled, and then only against the Kingdom or State and the subjects thereof, against which war has been so declared, and under such regulations as shall be established by the United States in Congress assembled, unless such State be infested by pirates, in which case vessels of war may be fitted out for that occasion, and kept so long as the danger shall continue or until the United States in Congress assembled shall determine otherwise.

VII.

When land forces are raised by any State for the common defense, all officers of or under the rank of colonel, shall be appointed by the legislature of each State respectively, by whom such forces shall be raised, or in such manner as such State shall direct, and all vacancies shall be filled up by the State which first made the appointment.

VIII.

All charges of war and all other expenses that shall be incurred for the common defense or general welfare, and allowed by the United States in Congress assembled, shall be defrayed out of a common treasury, which shall be supplied by the several States in proportion to the value of all land within each State, granted or surveyed for any person, as such land and the buildings and improvements thereon shall be estimated according to such mode as the United States in Congress assembled, shall from time to time direct and appoint.

The taxes for paying that proportion shall be laid and levied by the authority and direction of the legislatures of the several States within the time agreed upon by the United States in Congress assembled.

IX.

The United States in Congress assembled, shall have the sole and exclusive right and power of determining on peace and war, except in the cases mentioned in the sixth article; of sending and receiving ambassadors; entering into treaties and alliances, provided that no treaty of commerce shall be made whereby the legislative power of the respective States shall be restrained from imposing such imposts and duties on foreigners, as their own people are subjected to, or from prohibiting the exportation or importation of any species of goods or commodities whatsoever; of establishing rules for deciding in all cases, what captures on land or water shall be legal, and in what manner prizes taken by land or naval forces in the service of the United States shall be divided or appropriated; of granting letters of marque and reprisal in times of peace; appointing courts for the trial of piracies and felonies committed on the high seas and establishing courts for receiving and determining finally appeals in all cases of capture, provided that no member of Congress shall be appointed a judge of any of the said courts.

The United States in Congress assembled shall be the last resort on appeal in all disputes and differences now subsisting or that hereafter may arise between two or more States concerning boundary, jurisdiction, or any other causes whatever; which authority shall always be exercised in the manner following. Whenever the legislative or executive authority or lawful agent of any state in controversy with another shall present a petition to Congress stating the matter in question and praying for a hearing, notice thereof shall be given by order of Congress to the legislative or executive authority of the other

State in controversy, and a day assigned for the appearance of the parties by their lawful agents, who shall then be directed to appoint by joint consent, commissioners or judges to constitute a court for hearing and determining the matter in question; but if they cannot agree, Congress shall name three persons out of each of the United States, and from the list of such persons each party shall alternately strike out one, the petitioners beginning, until the number shall be reduced to thirteen; and from that number not less than seven, nor more than nine names as Congress shall direct, shall in the presence Congress be drawn out by lot, and the persons whose names shall be so drawn or any five of them, shall be commissioners or judges, to hear and finally determine the controversy, so always as a major part of the who shall hear the cause shall agree in the determination: and if either party shall neglect to attend at the day appointed, without showing reasons, which Congress shall judge sufficient, or being present shall refuse to strike, the Congress shall proceed to nominate three persons out of each State, and the secretary of Congress shall strike in behalf of such party absent or refusing; and the judgment and sentence of the court to be appointed, in the manner before prescribed, shall be final and conclusive; and if any of the parties shall refuse to submit to the authority of such court, or to appear or defend their claim or cause, the court shall nevertheless proceed to pronounce sentence, or judgment, which shall in like manner be final and decisive, the judgment or sentence and other proceedings being in either case transmitted to Congress, and lodged among the acts of Congress for the security of the parties concerned; provided that every commissioner, before he sits in judgment, shall take an oath to be administered by one of the judges of the supreme or superior court of the State, where the cause shall be tried, "well and truly to hear and determine the matter in question, according to the best of his judgment, without favor, affection or hope of reward": provided also, that no State shall be deprived of territory for the benefit of the United States.

All controversies concerning the private right of soil claimed under different grants of two or more States, whose jurisdictions as they may respect such lands, and the States which passed such grants are adjusted, the said grants or either of them being at the same time claimed to have originated antecedent to such settlement of jurisdiction, shall on petition of either party to the Congress of the United States, be finally determined as near as may be in the same manner as is before prescribed for deciding disputes respecting territorial jurisdiction between different States.

The United States in Congress assembled shall also have the sole and exclusive right and power of regulating the alloy and value of coin struck by their own authority, or by that of the respective States; fixing the standards of weights and measures throughout the United States; regulating the trade and managing all affairs with the Indians, not members of any of the States; provided that the legislative right of any State within its own limits will not be infringed or violated; establishing or regulating post offices from one State to another, throughout all the United States, and extracting such postage on the papers passing through the same as may be requisite to defray the expenses of said office; appointing all officers of the land forces, in the service of the United States, excepting regimental officers; appointing all officers of the naval forces, and commissioning all officers whatever in the service of the United States; making rules for the government and regulation of the said land and naval forces, and directing their operations.

The United States in Congress assembled shall have authority to appoint a committee, to sit in the recess of Congress, to be denominated "A Committee of the States," and to consist of one delegate from each State; and to appoint such other committees and civil officers as may be necessary for managing the general affairs of the United States under their direction—to appoint one of their members to preside, provided that no person be allowed to serve in the office of president more than one year in any term of three years; to ascertain the necessary sums of money to be raised for the service of the United States, and to appropriate and apply the same for defraying the public expenses; to borrow money, or emit bills of credit of the United States, transmitting every half-year to the respective States an account of the sums of money borrowed or emitted; to build and equip a navy; to agree upon the number of land forces, and to make requisitions from each State for its quota, in proportion to the number of white inhabitants in such State; which requisition shall be binding, and thereupon the legislature of each State shall appoint regimental officers, raise the men and cloath, arm and equip them in a soldier-like manner, at the expense of the United States; and the officers and men so cloathed, armed, and equipped shall march to the place appointed, and within the time agreed on by the United States in Congress assembled. But if the United States in Congress assembled shall, on consideration of circumstances judge proper that any State should not raise men, or should raise a smaller number of men than the quota thereof, such extra number shall be raised, officered, cloathed, armed, and equipped in the same manner as the quota of each State, unless the legislature of such State shall judge that such extra number cannot be safely spread out in the same, in which case they shall raise, officer, cloath, arm, and equip as many of such extra number as they judge can be safely spared. And the officers and men so cloathed, armed, and equipped, shall march to the place appointed, and within the time agreed on by the United States in Congress assembled.

The United States in Congress assembled shall never engage in a war, nor grant letters of marque or reprisal in time of peace, nor enter into any treaties or alliances, nor coin money, nor regulate the value thereof, nor ascertain the sums and expenses necessary for the defense and welfare of the United States, or any of them, nor emit bills, nor borrow money on the credit of the United States, nor appropriate money, nor agree upon the number of vessels of war, to be built or purchased, or the number of land or sea forces to be raised, nor appoint a commander in chief of the army or navy, unless nine States assent to the same; nor shall a question on any other point, except the adjourning from day to day be determined, unless by the votes of the majority of the United States in Congress assembled.

The Congress of the United States shall have the power to adjourn to any time within the year, and to any place within the United States, so that no period of adjournment be for a longer duration than the space of six months, and shall publish the journal of their proceedings monthly, except such parts thereof relating to treaties, alliances, or military operations, as in their judgment require secrecy; and the yeas and nays of the delegates of each State on any question shall be entered on the journal, when it is desired by any delegates of a State, or any of them, at his or their request shall be furnished with a transcript of the said journal, except such parts as are above excerpted, to lay before the legislatures of the several States.

X.

The Committee of the States, or any nine of them, shall be authorized to execute, in the recess of Congress, such of the powers of Congress as the United States in Congress assembled, by the consent of the nine States, shall from time to time think expedient to vest them with; provided that no power be delegated to the said Committee, for the exercise of which, by the Articles of Confederation, the voice of nine States in the Congress of the United States assembled the requisite.

XI.

Canada acceding to this confederation, and adjoining in the measures of the United States, shall be admitted into, and entitled to all the advantages of this Union; but no other colony shall be admitted into the same, unless such admission be agreed by nine States.

XII.

All bills of credit emitted, monies borrowed, and debts contracted by, or under the authority of Congress, before the assembling of the United States, in pursuance of the present confederation, shall be deemed and considered as a charge against the United States, for payment and satisfaction whereof the said United States, and the public faith are hereby solemnly pledged.

XIII.

Every State shall abide by the determination of the United States in Congress assembled, on all questions, which by this confederation are submitted to them. And the Articles of this Confederation shall be inviolably observed by every State, and the Union shall be perpetual; nor shall any alteration at any time hereafter be made in any of them; unless such alteration be agreed to in a Congress of the United States, and be afterwards confirmed by the legislatures of every State.

And Whereas it hath pleased the Great Governor of the World to incline the hearts of the legislatures we respectively represent in Congress, to approve of, and to authorize us to ratify the said Articles of Confederation and perpetual Union. Know Ye that we the undersigned delegates, by virtue of the power and authority to us given for that purpose, do by these presents, in the name and in behalf of our respective constituents, fully and entirely ratify and confirm each and every of the said Articles of Confederation and perpetual Union, and all and singular the matters and things therein contained: And we do further solemnly plight and engage the faith of our respective constituents, that they shall abide by the determinations of the United States in Congress assembled, on all questions, which by the said Confederation are submitted to them. And that the Articles thereof shall be inviolably observed by the States we respectively represent, and that the Union shall be perpetual.

In Witness whereof we have hereunto set our hands in Congress. Done at Philadelphia in the State of Pennsylvania the ninth day of July in the Year of our Lord One Thousand Seven Hundred and Seventy-eight, and the Third Year of the independence of America.

ANSWER KEY
SENATOR WORDSMART AND
THE CHOICE IS YOURS

Chapter One

A Minute with Senator WordSmart
Set # 1

1. c
2. g
3. d
4. a
5. e
6. b
7. f

The Choice Is Yours
Set # 1

1. c
2. c
3. a
4. c
5. d

A Minute with Senator WordSmart
Set # 2

1. e
2. b
3. d
4. a
5. c

A Minute with Senator WordSmart
Set # 3

1. e
2. c
3. b
4. d
5. g
6. f
7. a

The Choice Is Yours
Set # 2

1. d
2. b
3. d
4. b
5. d

Chapter Two

The Choice Is Yours
Set # 1

1. b
2. a
3. b
4. a
5. d

A Minute with Senator WordSmart
Set # 1

1. e
2. d
3. b
4. c
5. a

A Minute with Senator WordSmart
Set # 2

1. b
2. c
3. a
4. f
5. d
6. e

A Minute with Senator WordSmart
Set # 3

1. d
2. f
3. b
4. a
5. h
6. i
7. c
8. e
9. g

The Choice Is Yours
Set # 2

1. d
2. b
3. a
4. d
5. d

A Minute with Senator WordSmart
Set # 4

1. d
2. c
3. e
4. f
5. b
6. a

Chapter Three

A Minute with Senator WordSmart
Set # 1

1. g
2. f
3. b
4. d
5. h
6. c
7. e
8. a

The Choice Is Yours
Set # 1

1. a
2. d
3. c
4. b
5. d
6. d

A Minute with Senator WordSmart
Set # 2

1. d
2. f
3. i
4. c
5. h
6. g
7. a
8. e
9. b

The Choice Is Yours
Set # 2

1. d
2. d
3. a
4. c
5. b

A Minute with Senator WordSmart
Set # 3

1. c
2. d
3. a
4. e
5. b

The Choice Is Yours
Set # 3

1. a
2. d
3. c
4. a
5. c

Chapter Four

The Choice Is Yours
Set # 1

1. b
2. c
3. a
4. c
5. b

The Choice Is Yours
Set # 2

1. c
2. c
3. d
4. c
5. b

A Minute with Senator WordSmart
Set # 1

1. h
2. i
3. e
4. c
5. f
6. d
7. g
8. a
9. b

The Choice Is Yours
Set # 3

1. a
2. d
3. c
4. d
5. d

A Minute with Senator WordSmart
Set # 2

1. b
2. d
3. c
4. e
5. a

A Minute with Senator WordSmart
Set # 3

1. a
2. j
3. d
4. b
5. e
6. f
7. g
8. h
9. i
10. c

The Choice Is Yours
Set # 4

1. b
2. a
3. d
4. a
5. b

The Choice Is Yours
Set # 5

1. c
2. b
3. c
4. a
5. c

A Minute with Senator WordSmart
Set # 4

1. c
2. f
3. g
4. d
5. b
6. a
7. e
8. i
9. h

A Minute with Senator WordSmart
Set # 5

1. d
2. f
3. c
4. e
5. b
6. a

The Choice Is Yours
Set # 6

1. c
2. b
3. c,d
4. c
5. c

A Minute with Senator WordSmart
Set # 6

1. d
2. b
3. g
4. c
5. e
6. f
7. a

A Minute with Senator WordSmart
Set # 7

1. b
2. d
3. c
4. a
5. e

Chapter Five

A Minute with Senator WordSmart
Set # 1

1. c
2. g
3. e
4. f
5. b
6. a
7. d

The Choice Is Yours
Set # 1

1. a
2. a
3. b
4. d
5. d

A Minute with Senator WordSmart
Set # 2

1. d
2. e
3. f
4. a
5. b
6. c

A Minute with Senator WordSmart
Set # 3

1. e
2. d
3. c
4. b
5. a
6. g
7. f

The Choice Is Yours
Set # 2

1. c
2. b
3. c
4. b
5. c

The Choice Is Yours
Set # 3

1. b
2. a
3. d
4. b
5. a

The Choice Is Yours
Set # 4

1. c
2. d
3. a
4. d
5. a

A Minute with Senator WordSmart
Set # 4

1. e
2. b
3. d
4. c
5. a
6. f

The Choice Is Yours
Set # 5

1. c
2. b
3. d
4. d
5. b

A Minute with Senator WordSmart
Set # 5

1. c
2. g
3. a
4. f
5. h
6. d
7. b
8. e

Chapter Six

A Minute with Senator WordSmart
Set # 1

1. c
2. a
3. e
4. j
5. k
6. i
7. f
8. g
9. l
10. d
11. b
12. h

The Choice Is Yours
Set # 1

1. c
2. a
3. b
4. b
5. b

A Minute with Senator WordSmart
Set # 2

1. e
2. a
3. g
4. d
5. b
6. f
7. c

The Choice Is Yours
Set # 2

1. b
2. c
3. b
4. c
5. d

The Choice Is Yours
Set # 3

1. d
2. b
3. d
4. c
5. a

A Minute with Senator WordSmart
Set # 3

1. d
2. c
3. b
4. g
5. e
6. f
7. a
8. i
9. j
10. k
11. h

The Choice Is Yours
Set # 4

1. d
2. b
3. c
4. c
5. a

A Minute with Senator WordSmart
Set # 4

1. a
2. c
3. f
4. d
5. g
6. b
7. h
8. e

Chapter Seven

A Minute with Senator WordSmart
Set # 1

1. g
2. b
3. c
4. e
5. d
6. a
7. f

The Choice Is Yours
Set # 1

1. b
2. b
3. d
4. d
5. b

A Minute with Senator WordSmart
Set # 2

1. f
2. a
3. g
4. c
5. d
6. i
7. e
8. b
9. h

The Choice Is Yours
Set # 2

1. a
2. a
3. b
4. c
5. d

A Minute with Senator WordSmart
Set # 3

1. d
2. c
3. e
4. b
5. a

A Minute with Senator WordSmart
Set # 4

1. c
2. a
3. b
4. h
5. g
6. d
7. f
8. e

A Minute with Senator WordSmart
Set # 5

1. d
2. a
3. b
4. c
5. f
6. e

The Choice Is Yours
Set # 3

1. d
2. c
3. d
4. a
5. c

Chapter Eight

A Minute with Senator WordSmart
Set # 1

1. g
2. h
3. b
4. d
5. c
6. a
7. f
8. e

The Choice Is Yours
Set # 1

1. d
2. a
3. d
4. a
5. c

A Minute with Senator WordSmart
Set # 2

1. e
2. d
3. c
4. a
5. b

A Minute with Senator WordSmart
Set # 3

1. d
2. f
3. a
4. g
5. b
6. e
7. c

The Choice Is Yours
Set # 2

1. a
2. d
3. c
4. a
5. d

INDEX